EARLY FLYING MACHINES

{circa 1909}

Camden Miniature Steam Services.

Originally published by Thomas Nelson and Sons circa 1909

© Camden Miniature Steam Services 2003

British Library Cataloguing-in Publication-Data: a catalogue record of this book is held by the British Library.

First Printing 2003

ISBN No. 0-9536523-6-X

Published in Great Britain by:

Camden Miniature Steam Services
Barrow Farm, Rode, Frome, Somerset. BA11 6PS
Tel: 01373 - 830151
Fax: 01373 - 830516
www.camdenmin.co.uk

Camden stock one of the widest selections of engineering, technical and transportation book to be found Write to the above address for a copy of their latest Booklist.

Layout and Design by Camden Studios

Printed and Bound by Salisbury Printing Company

CONTENTS

Publisher's Note:

The contents of this book were originally published as six chapters in a four volume work entitled "Engineering Wonders of the World".

This is undated but circumstantial evidence, and especially the tables on pages 44 and 64, suggest it was published late in 1909. It is typical of the volumes of this type produced during the Victorian and Edwardian eras, being very informative and, as evidenced by the chapters reproduced here, assuming a reasonable level of technical understanding by the reader.

It would have been fascinating to know the author of this book, but none is given, although the whole work was edited by one Archibald Williams.

The contents have been rescanned, and improved where possible but, as far as is possible nearly one hundred years later, we have followed the layout of the original.

One hundred years ago the Wright Brothers made mans' first fully authenticated powered flight, triggering what must be the fastest technological advance that the human race has every made; when you can fly anywhere in the world in less than a day it is salutary to be reminded of the extent to which the Wright Brothers and the other pioneers of aviation were literally launching themselves into the unknown.

MECHANICAL FLIGHT AND AERIAL NAVIGATION.

INTRODUCTION.

As the beginning of the last century witnessed the development of steam locomotion by land and sea, and its last decade the rise of the gas-driven automobile, so are the first years of the twentieth century witnessing the growth of a means of transit which holds out greater possibilities than any of its predecessors. There is no need to review the many abortive strivings of man to emulate the way of a bird in the air - attempts which were doomed to failure because they ran far ahead of the mechanical science of the time. In human progress there has been, and always must be, an ordered sequence. The locomotive was an impossibility while tools were crude and the means of making rails in bulk not yet available. The growth of the petroleum industry, the invention of the pneumatic tyre and of the internal combustion engine, and the existence of good roads, prepared the way for the motor car. And now we seem to have reached a period when, thanks to mechanical skill and scientific knowledge, the solution of the problems of aerial navigation cannot be delayed much longer. Though critics may scoff, facts are facts; and among the facts with which they have to reckon are that men *have* travelled hundreds of miles in dirigible balloons, and that men *have* flown on self-lifting machines for long distances at high speeds.

Success seems to have come quite suddenly. In 1852, Henry Giffard devised an airship that propelled itself at a low velocity; in 1884, Renard and Krebs produced one that proved considerably more successful; in 1900, Count Zeppelin first moved a dirigible with the aid of a petrol engine; in 1902, Santos Dumont won the Deutsch Prize with a short flight round the Eiffel Tower. These achievements sum up the progress made till seven years ago. To-day, dirigible balloons are numerous; flying machines that *can* fly are to be counted by the score, and their number increases every week.

We must not forget, however, that the feats recently accomplished are the outcome of a great amount of experiment in the laboratory and in the open air. There has been little of what may be called accidental discovery in the story of the aeroplane. Slowly and systematically, with the aid of a multitude of models, the laws of the air have been explored, the problems of maintaining stability partly solved. If progress has been, on the whole, much slower than in the case of the steam locomotive, the steamship, and the electric and petrol-driven vehicle, it is due mainly to the characteristic difficulties of aerial navigation, the main one being that the failure of any man-carrying apparatus is attended by the most serious consequences, financial and physical. This meant a cautious advance into the fascinating field of aeronautics. A lot of work was done without achieving results such as would appeal to the popular imagination. Experimenters were regarded as fools, bent on breaking their necks. Arguments were marshalled to show that man was not intended to fly, and that therefore he should not endeavour to do so. It might have been maintained with equal fairness that man was not designed to travel on land at a hundred miles an hour, or on the sea at almost half that speed. The prejudice which overlooked these counter-arguments was based in no small degree upon an ignorance about or misconception of the physical qualities of the atmosphere. Though at rest, the air seems to have no substance, the hurricane - air moving at high velocity - makes playthings of solid structures. It shows a curious anomaly of thought that, while the dirigible balloon was regarded as foredoomed to failure as being unable to overcome air resistance, the flying machine should have been derided on the grounds that mere air would not serve for its support. The fundamental fact that air will give support to any mass if that mass be provided with suitable surfaces and be propelled at a sufficiently high speed is now, however, more generally recognised.

Though veritable engineering wonders, the airship and the flying machine are still in their infancy, so young that we cannot yet see clearly what form they are likely to take as they develop. Will the final victory rest with the dirigible balloon or with the heavier-than-air self-lifting and self-supporting machine? Or will there be uses found for both types of air craft? It is impossible to say.

The attitude which scouts the idea of aviation becoming more than a sport for the wealthy few seems hardly worthy of serious consideration. The advantages of being able to travel through the air, upborne by a medium which requires not a farthing's-worth of expenditure in repairs, and which is practically illimitable, are too obvious to need setting forth. The motor car has come into general use largely because of its capacity to save time in "cross-country" journeys, through districts not served by the railway. But even the car has to keep to the beaten track; to cross a river at one or other of a few points - often many miles apart - at which bridges have been built; to traverse mountain ranges where the engineers have made the roads. Long detours are, in many circumstances, unavoidable. The aeroplane and "dirigible" know no such limitations. Given the capacity to keep moving in the direction desired, there will be nothing to hinder them getting from any one place to any other.

What effects the new locomotion will have on society it is indeed difficult to foresee.

Pessimists, directing their attention mainly to the combative instincts of mankind, croak of aerial invasion and warfare in the clouds. The military side of aerial navigation has been, we venture to think, too widely emphasized. The locomotive has played a most important part in modern warfare, yet its mission has been mainly peaceful. Similarly, though the airship, like the submarine boat in another element, will be employed in war time on account of the moral effect produced by its possible presence, it will justify itself far more fully as a means of maintaining communication in many parts of the world whither roads and railway have not yet penetrated. Consider what an aerial postal service would mean to people living on the outskirts of civilisation, in districts where pioneers are at present painfully feeling their way.

In the following chapters we are concerned, not with questions of the future, but with the past and present progress of aeronautics. We shall review the principles and problems of mechanical flight, and give attention to the most successful aeroplanes of today. The aeronautical engine, upon the development of which has depended so largely that of human flight, is treated in a separate article. The second main section is devoted to the airship or dirigible balloon.

Things are moving so fast, metaphorically as well as literally, in the field of aeronautics that we cannot hope to keep here quite abreast of the latest developments. Even while these articles pass through the press fresh triumphs will doubtless be won. The letterpress and illustrations will, however, have a value, even where they do not refer to principles rather than applications, as embodying a record of the early chapters in the history of the most fascinating, as it is the most recent, of engineering wonders.

A WRIGHT BIPLANE IN FLIGHT.

(Photo, Illustrations Bureau.)

THE THEORY AND PRINCIPLES
OF THE AEROPLANE

THE physical laws governing the successful operation of an aeroplane are at the present time still being explored. Much valuable research work has been done by Lilienthal, Chanute, Maxim, Phillips, Lanchester, Langley, the Wrights, and others; and conclusions, capable of experimental proof, have been arrived at, so that human flight has moved from the position of mere aspiration into the region of accomplished fact. A great deal remains to be done, however, before man will rival the birds in this latest form of locomotion.

The scientific literature dealing with aerostatics is as yet comparatively scanty, and of a nature which may well scare the unscientific reader. It is our desire to avoid here tiresome technicalities, formulae, and equations, and to present, in as simple a form as possible, the physical facts and problems with which experimenters have to deal.

Most of us have handled the toy kite, a very simple apparatus which is subservient to essentially the same laws as the aeroplane. When a kite is launched in a wind sufficiently strong to lift it at all, it speedily rises to a certain elevation, at which it remains so long as the velocity of the wind does not change. The steadiness of the **THE KITE.** kite implies an equilibrium of the forces acting upon it. These forces, as shown in Fig. 1, are: G, gravity, which remains practically unaltered under all conditions; W, the pressure of the wind, acting perpendicularly to the oblique surface of the kite; and P, the pull of the string.

The force W may be resolved into two other forces. One of these, known as *drift*, tends to move the kite horizontally in the direction of the wind; the other, called *lift*, to raise the kite vertically in opposition to gravity. In practice, if not in theory, the drift is augmented by the direct resistance offered by edges, excrescences, and roughnesses of the kite.

If the wind sinks, the kite sinks also, increasing its angle with the horizontal. This causes it to capture and force downwards more and more air until a state of equilibrium is again attained. We must observe, however, that this increase of angle means also a great increase in drift proportionately to lift. If the descent of the kite had been caused, not by decrease in wind velocity, but by the addition of weight to the kite, the increase in the pull on the string would have been very noticeable.

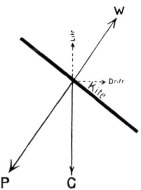

Fig. 1. - DIAGRAM TO SHOW THE FORCES ACTING ON A KITE.

It is the aim of the kite-maker as well as of the aeroplane builder to design surfaces which shall use the wind pressure most efficiently - that is, extract a maximum of lifting force, and be subject to a minimum of drift.

If the string of the kite breaks, the equilibrium of forces is destroyed; drift and gravity take command, and the kite either tumbles or glides to earth backwards. If it were possible to attach to the kite at the moment of rupture a weightless engine and propeller, exerting a horizontal windward push equal to the drift, the kite would remain stationary.

Again, were the wind to drop suddenly, and the engine to give the kite a forward velocity equal to that of the wind, the kite would move forward - assuming that it were able to maintain its stability - and be a true aeroplane or self-supporting heavier-than-air apparatus. Under usual conditions a kite is not strictly self-supporting, in that it depends on the resistance of a string anchored to a fixed point.

Lilienthal, the great German experimenter, Octave Chanute, the brothers Wright, and other seekers after aerostatical knowledge, made use of man-bearing "gliders", either free or anchored, of large area, as well as of laboratory tests on surfaces of various forms, from which was derived the preliminary knowledge necessary to the construction of mechanical self-propelled and self-sustaining machines. Without going into wearisome details, it may be stated that the shape and the arrangement of surfaces to give the greatest lifting power and stability were the chief objects of their search.

It was proved conclusively that (*a*) a true plane had not, area for area, so great a sustaining power as a slightly curved surface, convex on the upper side. Horatio Phillips, and sub-

SHAPE OF SUPPORTING SURFACES.

sequently Maxim, demonstrated by elaborate tests that (*b*) an aeroplane (we here apply the term to a sustaining surface, not to a machine) with the upper surface more curved than the lower, and inclining downwards in front so as to give a "negative

Fig 2. - SECTION OF A DECK WHICH GIVES GOOD LIFTING POWER.
The arrows indicate the direction of the wind.

entering angle" (see Fig. 2), was most efficient. Tests showed that (*c*) depth fore and aft was not so important as length of transverse entering edge; that, in fact, a number of narrow aeroplanes, arranged one over the other, Venetian blind fashion, were much more effective than a single aeroplane of equal length and of a breadth totalling that of the narrow aeroplanes. It has been established that (*d*) in the case of well-made aeroplanes the lift increases, within certain limits, in direct proportion to the angle of inclination or incidence: thus, a plane making an angle of 10° with the horizontal has twice the lift of one inclined at 5° to the horizontal. Also that (e) the drift varies, within certain limits, relatively to the lift with the angle of inclination: thus, an aeroplane set at an angle of 1 in 12 (that is, having the forward edge 1 inch higher than the rear edge for every foot of width) develops twelve times as much lift as drift. Also that (f) the lift increases as the *square* of the velocity of motion relatively to the air:

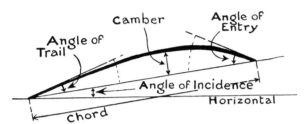

Fig. 3. - DIAGRAM TO EXPLAIN TERMS "ANGLE OF INCIDENCE", "ANGLE OF ENTRY", "CAMBER", ETC.

therefore the higher the speed, the smaller the angle of the plane needed to sustain a given weight, and the greater the lifting effect in proportion to the power employed. This fact is due to the inertia of the air, and has its analogy in the fact that a skater travelling fast will be supported by ice that would not bear him at rest.

The cause of the great lifting power of a curved aeroplane with a downward-pointing front edge is not yet

AIR ACTION. clearly understood. Phillips advanced the theory that the upward push given to the air by the front edge creates a partial vacuum over the upper rear portion of the aeroplane. Maxim, on the other hand, has recorded his opinion that the air follows the upper curve and joins that passing along the underneath surface at the trailing edge, giving a resultant upward push. Whatever the correct explanation may be, the curved section is used generally, the ribs in some cases being tapered and covered on both sides, so as to make the curvature more pronounced on the top than on the bottom; in others, covered on the lower side only. There seems to be a lack of standardisation in this respect at present.

As the lifting power of a flying machine increases, other things being equal, with its bearing surfaces, and is augmented by increasing the length of forward edge of these surfaces, as wide **DISPOSITION OF PLANES.** a spread as possible is, in this respect, a desideratum. The spread must, however, be limited to convenient dimensions. Hence one section of experimenters have adopted the *biplane*, with two "decks" set one above the other at a distance apart at least equal to the width of the decks, and a few have tried the *triplane* and *multiplane*. Blériot, Latham, and others have chosen the alternative of the monoplane, having a single deck subdivided into two wings, one on each side of a central "body". From the constructional point of view, the biplane has the advantage of admitting a girder-like form of cross bracing between the two decks, and enabling the propeller or propellers to be mounted conveniently behind the decks, where, by virtue of acting on air already disturbed, they prove more efficient than the monoplane's tractor screw, which bites air previously undisturbed, and drives it back on to the body it is moving. Yet the performances of the monoplane have been so satisfactory as regards speed that one is driven to the conclusion that as yet it is too early to dogmatize on the respective merits of the two types.

We may digress here for a moment to introduce and explain the term "aspect ratio" now commonly used in describing the shape of a deck. An **ASPECT RATIO.** aspect ratio of 6 to 1, for example, implies that the greatest length from end to end is six times the greatest depth from the front to the rear edge.

From what has been said already, it will be deduced that the ability of a flying machine to keep in the air depends on (1) the design of the supporting surfaces; (2) the area of the supporting surfaces; (3) the inclination of the supporting surfaces; (4)

the speed of travel, which in turn is dependent on the motive force. When travelling horizontally, the machine is practically constantly climbing a slope equal to that of the natural gliding angle of descent which it takes to earth when the engines are stopped. So that in effect the power required to sustain it must be equivalent to the extra power (above that developed on the level) needed to drive a motor car of equal weight at an equal speed up an incline equal to the gliding angle of

THE DESIGN OF A FLYING MACHINE.

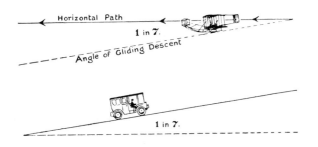

Fig. 4. - An aeroplane travelling horizontally has, weight for weight, to exert as much force to support itself as is required to propel a motor car up an incline having a gradient equal to the gliding angle of the aeroplane.

the aeroplane, and, in addition, to overcome the air resistance and skin friction of all parts of the machine. The first factor, the aerodynamic resistance, is decreased relatively to the lift by higher speed, since, as we have seen already, the lift increases with the speed; the second factor, head resistance, increases in the same ratio, as the square of the velocity. Hence one factor tends to counterbalance the other. It follows from this that for any one machine there is a certain speed at which it will support itself and travel from one point to another most economically - that is, with the least expenditure of force. To improve the speed without increasing the power or altering the weight, the head resistance must be diminished, or the design of the decks improved and the inclination reduced. Should the designer elect rather to decrease the supporting area without increasing

engine power, he would be compelled to increase also the inclination of the decks - and with it the "drift" - which would tend to diminish speed - a very undesirable alternative.

An aeroplane must travel at a certain speed to support itself at all. To enable it to rise, the power must be increased. Merely to point an elevating rudder upwards will not suffice, as the increase of inclination will increase the "drift" of the supporting surfaces and slow the machine. At the great meeting at Rheims the struggles of competitors to reach the highest altitude - the winner rose but slightly more than 500 ft. - proved the difficulty of increasing the steepness of ascent over and above the angle which the machine must take to maintain a horizontal path.

An efficient machine has a gliding angle of about 1 in 8; that is, when influenced by gravity alone, it will descend one foot for every 8 ft. it progresses.

The power needed to propel the machine on a horizontal course is that required to, say, roll a ball of equal weight up a frictionless incline of 1 in 8, and also to overcome frictionless air resistance. To maintain stability a speed of from 35 to 40 m.p.h. is required.

Let us assume that the machine weighs 500 lbs. with pilot, and that it has to travel at 40 m.p.h. to sustain itself. Every second 500 lbs. will be lifted (in *effect*) ⅛th of 60 ft. = 7½ ft. To effect this will require about 7½ **POWER NEEDED FOR AN AEROPLANE.** horse-power. In order to rise, at least one fifth more power must be added, making 9 horse-power in all. Owing to loss of power in transmission and to screw inefficiency, we must allow a further 30 per cent. The engine for a 500 lb. load should therefore develop some 16 horse-power, or about 1 horse-power for every 31 lbs. of weight.

The fact that some flying machines give a much better lift per horse-power is due to a naturally better (more acute) gliding angle, to good design as regards minimizing frictional resistances, to high engine and propeller efficiency, or to a combination of all three. A Wright machine, weighing 950 lbs., is propelled at 40 m.p.h. by a 24 horse-power engine, which works out at over 40 lbs. carried per horse-power.

THE MAINTENANCE OF STABILITY

The flying machine, as at present constituted, is able and liable to topple in any direction. As flight necessitates high speed and considerable elevation above the earth's surface, the maintenance of stability is literally of vital importance. Even under favourable conditions early experimenters found it extremely difficult to counteract the tendency of a glider or power-driven machine to execute unpremeditated dives and somersaults. The history of flight is punctuated by records of more or less disastrous spills resulting directly from the failure of the aviator to keep the machine in such a position that the centre of air pressure should lie over or coincide with the centre of gravity of the mass in motion.

The problem of balancing an aeroplane is a peculiar one. Hold a sheet of paper horizontally, and let it fall. It darts first one way and then another. You can only guess at the direction it will take finally before alighting. If launched horizontally, it behaves in a most erratic manner. Even a more scientifically designed paper "glider", instead of following a steady downward course, dips up and down as if influenced by a horizontal rudder. This phenomenon is due to the fact that the pressure on a surface moving obliquely through the air varies in strength at different points on that surface, being greater at the front than at the back edge. The centre of pressure - that is, the point at which the total pressure may be

THE CENTRE OF PRESSURE.

considered to act - is normally situated, in the case of a curved "deck", about one third of the width of the deck from its front edge; or the pressure may be drawn transversely through this point.

An increase of speed moves the centre of pressure nearer to the front edge of the oblique surface; a decrease causes it to recede towards the rear edge. A paper glider, as it swoops downwards, is tilted up in front because, though the centre of gravity remains unchanged, the centre of pressure has worked forwards, and the air gets an upward leverage at the front. The tilt gives the glider extra lift, but also slows it; the speed decreases, the centre of pressure recedes, and the original angle of descent is resumed. This cycle of variations may recur many times in the course of a glide.

To keep an aeroplane from pitching longitudinally, provision must be made whereby the centre of pressure may be kept close to the centre of gravity at varying speeds. All biplanes are fitted with an auxiliary movable horizontal surface or surfaces in front of the main decks, and under the control of the pilot. Movements of the elevator vary the average angle of incidence of all the sustaining surfaces. Thus, if the aeroplane is gliding downwards, and the pilot wishes to take a horizontal course, he raises the front edge of the elevator. This gives the elevator a greater upward leverage, and increases the angle of incidence of the main decks. To cause a descent, the elevator is tilted downwards, and the general angle of incidence decreased. Gusts of winds coming headways on are counteracted by a proper manipulation of the elevator. It should be understood, however, that the elevator has but little effect in making the machine take a steady upward course. For this, an increase in the motive force is required.

FRONT ELEVATORS.

The Wrights depend entirely on the front elevator for the maintenance of fore

(*Photo, Illustrations Bureau.*)

HENRY FARMAN CARRYING A PASSENGER ON HIS BIPLANE.

and aft stability. They have expressed the opinion that, as the cyclist must learn to balance his cycle, so the aviator must learn to balance is aeroplane. At first the task is not easy, but practice brings a habit of doing the right thing without conscious calculation.

That the lesson can be learnt without great difficulty - at least by persons naturally receptive - has been proved by events. Yet there is much to be said in favour of *automatic* stability systems, which tend to relieve the pilot of the strain entailed by constant watchfulness. In fact, it is hard to conceive what one may style the successful commercial flying machine of the future as a contrivance which will be kept right way up only by virtue of the pilot's unceasing vigilance.

AUTOMATIC STABILITY.

The Voisin, Farman, and some other biplanes carry a horizontal immovable tail in the rear in addition to a front elevator; while monoplanes of all patterns have a horizontal tail as well as a horizontal rudder, which, in the case of these machines, could not well be placed ahead of the main decks, owing to the position of the tractor screw. The tail checks sudden alterations of angle, and generally tends to keep the aeroplane level. A rear horizontal rudder is, however, not so efficient as the front elevator, as it has little effect in checking the speed of the aeroplane when the latter alights. A front elevator is turned up somewhat abruptly just before the machine touches ground, and diminishes the speed while flattening the angle of descent, so that a well-handled aeroplane alights without shock. The action is very similar to that of a bird throwing its head back and opposing its wings almost square-ly to the air just as it reaches earth. The monoplane, with its rear elevator, which has little braking effect, is

FIXED TAILS.

apt to come down heavily and damage the wheeled carriage and the propeller. Thanks, however, to its tail, it has good longitudinal stability if the weight be properly distributed. At one time it was thought that its stability was far inferior to that of the biplane, but M. Blériot, after many experiments, succeeded in overcoming the diving propensities of this type.

REAR ELEVATORS.

Against the tail it may be urged that it decreases speed. The American biplane, the *June Bug*, originally carried a tail. When this was removed the speed was greatly increased. We may observe, too, that the biplanes with double-decked tails are not a speedy class. On the other hand, the monoplane type of tail does not appear to militate against speed.

Though it is as yet early to dogmatize on points relating to aeroplane design, it may be assumed that the tail increases longitudinal stability, but that the front control is extremely valuable. The tailless biplane is more "handy" and easy to manoeuvre; the tailed machine more stable, but less easily swung about.

To counteract sideways tilting several systems have been used. The first was to turn the two halves of a deck upwards to form a "dihedral angle" at the middle. This gave stability, but caused a rolling from side to side. The straight-edged deck is somewhat less stable, but is free from rolling. Decks with drooping ends have been used by Mr. Cody, those on his aeroplane having a dip of several inches towards the tips. A partridge when gliding droops its wings, but keeps remarkably steady, so that possibly the third form may prove the most suitable. At present the straight deck is in vogue. A very slight dihedral angle is used on the Antoinette monoplanes, as previously by Langley on his model aerodrome, and by Maxim for his big steam-driven machine.

LATERAL STABILITY.

The Voisin biplanes are provided with vertical curtains situated between the main decks and the upper and lower planes of the tail. Monoplanes usually have one or more vertical fins attached to the framework of the rear part of the body. These devices belong to the automatic class, and may be compared to the fins on a torpedo or the deep keel of a sailing ship.

VERTICAL CURTAINS.

Though the permanent shape of deck and the employment of curtains and fins may help to prevent tilting, they cannot correct it when it occurs. For this purpose, it is necessary to use auxiliary planes attached to the decks or tail, or to alter temporarily the shape of the decks themselves - to "warp" them, as it is now termed. The Wrights warp both main decks by means of a device which will be explained on a later page, bending downwards the end of the deck which is lowest and thereby increasing the lift at that end. To prevent the resulting drag slewing the aeroplane round, the warping mechanism is linked up with the rudder, and moves it simultaneously to the side away from the warped end.

AUXILIARY DEVICES.

The wings of the Blériot monoplane are warped in a somewhat similar manner. The Farman biplane and the Antoinette monoplane have "ailerons", or flaps, attached to the rear edges of the main decks. (See Figs. 4 and 8, pages 23 and 28.) Cody uses a front elevator, the two halves of which can be moved in opposing directions, as well as small balancing planes between the main decks.

On the whole, the problem of maintaining stability has been solved in a considerable degree. This is proved by the fact that the difficulties of balancing a well-designed aeroplane are soon overcome by a clever learner. One of the most remarkable features of the development of aviation has been the sudden rise to fame of aviators after but a few weeks of practice. We must not forget, however, that even the hardiest pilot will not venture forth in rough weather; that the aeroplane is as yet a fair weather machine, which cannot be depended upon to keep steady if struck by a squall, however skilfully handled.

The Wrights, though advocates of the "pilot-balanced" machine, have applied for a patent covering a mechanical device for maintaining automatic stability. In this the human brain is replaced by the pressure of air on a plane as regards longitudinal, and by the movements of a pendulum as regards lateral stability. Compressed air is substituted for muscular action. The plane and pendulum open valves which admit compressed air to an engine operating the elevator and the rudder and warping mechanism. The apparatus has not, so far as is known, been subjected to any actual tests, but it may play a part in the future of aviation.

MECHANICAL STABILITY.

The gyroscope has been used successfully on the Whitehead torpedo to maintain direction, and on small vessels to prevent rolling. Also, the Brennan monorail railway carriage is balanced entirely by means of a gyroscope. It is thought that the same mechanism might be of use for stabilising an aeroplane, if arranged so as not to cause too violent strains in the machine. A combination of gyroscope and pendulum has been proposed, whereby the decks or auxiliary planes could be warped or deflected automatically to maintain equilibrium.

THE GYROSCOPE.

Another solution of the problem lies in high speed. The faster a body moves, the less easily it is diverted from its path or turned about on itself. A bicycle driven at twenty miles an hour requires no steering, whereas only an expert could balance the bicycle, without the use of his hands, at walking pace. Similarly, an aeroplane

SPEED AND STABILITY.

moving at a hundred miles an hour would be practically unaffected by strong gusts of wind, and not be liable to tilt either longitudinally or transversely. Such a speed would, however, imply the use of small lifting surfaces, which in turn would make landing a difficult matter.

Possibly invention may devise some method of altering the area of the decks at will - of reefing them, as it were, during flight, and unreefing when the time comes to alight. It must be confessed that the aeroplane of today does not appear to lend itself to any such system as this.

TUNING UP AN ANTOINETTE MONOPLANE PREPARATORY TO A FLIGHT.
(Photo, Illustrations Bureau.)

S.F. CODY CROSSING THE BASINGSTOKE CANAL.   *(Photo, Topical.)*

He is holding his hands over his head to show the stability of his machine.

THREE VOISIN MACHINE BIPLANES AT THE STARTING-LINE, RHEIMS.   *(Photo, Illustrations Bureau.)*

FLYING MACHINES OF TODAY

A REVIEW OF SOME OF THE MOST SUCCESSFUL TYPES, WITH DETAILED DESCRIPTIONS OF THEIR CHIEF FEATURES

FROM the theory of the flying machine we may now turn to the most prominent examples of its practical application. Inasmuch as at the time of writing the successful heavier-than-air machines are of one or other of two types - the biplanes and monoplanes - we shall not make reference here to the triplanes, multiplanes, helicopters, and flapping machines which are still in the purely experimental stage.

In the present article, the term flying machine is synonymous with aeroplane. "Aeroplane" is not a happy term in itself, because planes seldom form part of a flying machine, whereas the curved or cambered deck is always used, at least for the main sustaining surfaces. However, as the word "aeroplane" has established itself, and conveys a distinct impression of a certain type of machine, it must stand.

The dimensions of various machines given in the following paragraphs may be found to differ slightly from the figures given in other publications. This may be explained by the fact that minor alterations are constantly being made by the designers and that several machines of the same pattern may vary among themselves in detail. It is possible that before these words appear in print, some of the aeroplanes described may have undergone considerable modifications, as the result of experience suggesting improvements.

THE WRIGHT MACHINE

When the history of the development of the heavier-than-air machine comes to be written, the Wright brothers will occupy a position in it analogous to that of George Stephenson in the history of the locomotive. As Stephenson first produced a really practicable locomotive capable of prolonged effort and high speed, so can the Wrights claim to have built the first really practicable flying machine.

The story of the Wrights' struggle to master the air has been told sufficiently often to render unnecessary here anything more than a brief *résumé*. The preliminary experiments were begun in 1896, and continued until 1903. During this period were built many

EXPERIMENTS WITH GLIDERS.

double-decked "gliders", modelled on the lines laid down by Lilienthal and Chanute; the laws of balance were explored; the efficiency of curves with regard to lift and drift examined; and a large number of glides were made, the longest being over 600 ft. long, and lasting 26 seconds. The glider used for this particular flight had a

preceding glider.

The best performance put up during the year was half a mile in just under a minute at a speed of about 30 miles per hour. The lift obtained approximated to 60 lbs. per horse-power developed by the engine.

The next year the Wrights shifted the scene of operations from the neighbour-

COUNT LAMBERT ON A WRIGHT AEROPLANE.   *(Photo, Illustrations Bureau.)*

supporting area of 312 square feet, a span of 35 ft., and a weight of 117 lbs.

In 1903 the brothers considered that they had collected sufficient data to justify the application of a petrol motor to a new glider specially built. The engine, built by themselves, had four cylinders of 4-inch bore and stroke, weighed 250 lbs., and developed 12 horse-power at 1,000 revolutions per minute. To support the extra weight, the decks of this machine were given an area about double that of the

hood of Chesapeake Bay - where the prevailing winds had been particularly favourable for gliding experiments - to their home at Dayton, in Ohio, and proceeded to build a second machine. With this - driven by a 17 horse-power engine - they

AN ENGINE FITTED.

made many flights, the record for the year being rather more than 3 miles in 5 minutes 17 seconds, at a speed of 34 miles per hour. They also had the satisfaction of completing an aerial circuit for the first time.

Encouraged by their success, the Wrights built, in 1905, the now famous "White Flier" - the "Rocket" of aviation. This machine had a deck area of 625 square feet, and mounted a 24 horse-power 250-lb. gasolene engine, which drove two large wooden propellers, 6 feet in diameter, in opposite directions, by means of chain gearing. The weight of the machine "mounted" - that is, with pilot "up" - totalled 925 lbs.

During the months of September and **THE FIRST GREAT HUMAN FLIGHTS.** October the "White Flier" made some remarkable journeys, all the more remarkable from the fact that three years elapsed before they were beaten by those of any other machine. The following is the record:-

DATE	DISTANCE	TIME
September 26, 1905	11⅛ miles	18 min. 9 sec.
September 29, 1905	12 miles	19 min. 55 sec.
October 3, 1905	15½ miles	25 min. 5 sec.
October 4, 1905	21 miles	33 min. 17 sec.
October 5, 1905	24½ miles	38 min. 3 sec.

Owing to the privacy with which the flights were conducted and to the silence of the local press, the performances were generally discredited in France, where Captain Ferber, Gabriel Voisin, and M. Ernest Archdeacon had for some years been following up the gliding experiments of Lilienthal and Octave Chanute. Sufficient independent testimony was forthcoming, however, to establish as a matter beyond doubt that the Wright aeroplane had flown with a passenger for a considerable distance, had executed flights in any direction desired, and had come safely to ground at high and low speeds; that, in short, there was no reason to disbelieve the statements recorded by the Wrights.

During 1906 public curiosity compelled the brothers to content themselves with improving the smaller details of a machine which they considered to have a commercial value. In 1907 they made several flights, and opened negotiations with several Governments for the sale of their invention, and in the following year brought their Flier to France. After some preliminary tuning-up flights, Wilbur Wright stayed in the air for 19 mins. 48⅖ secs., on September 5th, 1908. On the 21st, he broke his own record handsomely with a flight lasting 1 hr. 31 mins. 25⅘ **RECORD-BREAKING IN FRANCE.** secs., and caused a tremendous increase of popular interest in aviation. Two months later he travelled 62 miles in 1 hr. 54 mins. 53⅖ secs.; and on the last day of the year won the Michelin Trophy with a flight which lasted 2 hrs. 20 mins. 23⅓ secs., and covered a distance of 77½ miles. (This was the officially measured distance. The actual distance travelled was considerably greater.)

These really astonishing feats, which remained unbeaten for seven months[*], resulted in orders for Wright aeroplanes being placed by several Governments, and many private individuals, and at the present moment more machines of this type exist than any other. A description of its main features will therefore be of interest.

The decks are about 40 ft. long and 6½ ft. deep from front to rear, giving a total bearing surface of about 530 square feet (in some of the most recent machines the surface has **THE MACHINE.** been reduced considerably). The framework of each deck consists of two parallel main cross members - one running along the front edge, the other about 4 ft. 3 ins. in the rear - and connected at the ends. These support arched ribs, 15 ins. apart, slightly curved, and composed of upper and lower slats separated by blocks and approaching nearer to one another towards the back edge. They pass round the after cross member. Above and beneath the ribs is fastened rubbered cloth, to form a double-surfaced deck.

[*]On August 7th, 1909, M. Sommer flew for 2 hrs. 27 mins. 15 secs., on a Farman biplane, to be in turn beaten by Henry Farman (on a Farman biplane) on August 27th, with a flight lasting 3 hrs. 4 mins. 56⅖ secs., (180 kms. = 112 miles).

The two decks are held apart by a number of wooden uprights attached to the cross members of the decks. The three rear supports at each end are merely hooked on, so as to allow for a small amount of movement. The whole structure of the body is suitably stayed with diagonal wires to form a truss.

action. A lever (R) on the pilot's right hand is connected by a bar (A) to the rudder gearing, and pivoted at the bottom as regards forwards and backwards motion on the end of a rod (B), which can be revolved sideways in sockets. At the rear end of this rod is a short

HOW THE DECKS ARE WARPED.

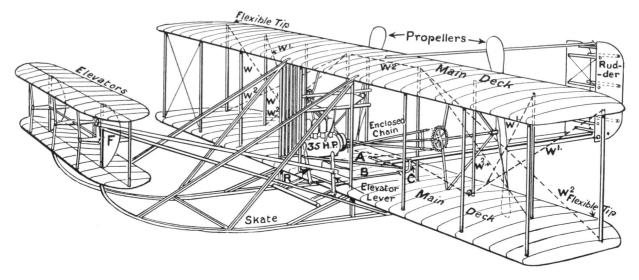

Fig. 1. - DIAGRAM SHOWING THE VARIOUS PARTS OF THE WRIGHT AEROPLANE,
AND THE METHOD OF WARPING THE DECKS.

About 8½ ft. to the rear of the main decks are two vertical rudders for lateral steering, 2 ft. wide and nearly 6 ft. high. Cross-spars link them together. For vertical steering and balancing, a couple of horizontal planes are mounted 10 ft. or so in front of the main decks, similarly interconnected and pivoted on vertical extensions of the long skates on which the machine rests. Between the planes are two semicircular fixed planes to assist in the maintenance of stability. A lever, held in the pilot's left hand, controls the elevation rudders.

STEERING AND BALANCING PLANES.

The most interesting feature of the Wright machines is the device for warping the wings, either independently of or in conjunction with the movements of the steering rudders. The accompanying diagram (Fig. 1) will assist to explain its

vertical arm (C) from the top of which wires (W¹W¹) run right and left several feet along the upper side of the bottom planes, and then pass upwards through pulleys to the tops of the rear wooden uprights at the ends of the decks. Sideways movements of the lever R flex downwards one or other end of both decks. A secondary series of wires (W²W²) connecting the bottoms of the end uprights via the underside of the top decks cause a reverse flexure at the other end of the decks. Thus, if the lever be put over to the left, the right tips are drawn down and the left tips bent up. By this simple system, which is largely responsible for the "handiness" of the Wright machines, the pilot is enabled to make the decks assist the rudder, or the rudder assist the decks, for preserving balance and for rounding curves. The reader will have no difficulty in understanding that the downward flexing of one end of a deck will make that end rise and lose speed, and that the flattening of the other end will diminish "lift" and increase speed. While counteracting a tilt the drag put on one side slews the machine on its vertical axis, and this has to be counteracted by a simultaneous moving of the steering rudders in the proper direction. Again, the rounding of a curve with the assistance of the rudder alone would produce an extra lift at the outside end, where the speed is greatest; and here the ability to flex the inside end downwards

of the body are found a couple of long wooden runners or skates, which prove extremely efficient for absorbing the shocks of landing. Preparatory to a flight the machine is placed on a wooden trolley having two small wheels tandem, running on a rail about 23 yards long. Behind the machine, and in line with the rail, is a wooden tower, inside which are a number of iron discs weighing about 1,500 lbs. From the discs a rope

HOW THE MACHINE IS STARTED.

A
WRIGHT AEROPLANE
ON
THE STARTING-RAIL.

In the rear is the tower with weight discs raised. To the right of the machine is the carriage on which it is moved to the starting-rail after a descent.

(Photo, Topical.)

comes in useful. Primarily, the flexure is for the purpose of stability; incidentally, it assists steering.

The four-cylinder engine, which is described in another place, transmits its power to twin-screw propellers behind the decks through chains, one crossed so that the propellers shall revolve in opposite directions. The indirect drive is taken advantage of to use large propellers turning at a little more than a quarter of the speed of the engine. Two screws, working in opposite directions, assist stability by eliminating all gyroscopic action.

ENGINE AND PROPELLERS.

The Wrights still adhere to their original system of starting their machine by means of external help. In place of the usual wheeled carriage attached to the underside

passes over a pulley in the tower top, down the tower, under a pulley at the base, along the ground to a pulley at the far end of the rail, and back towards the carriage, to which it can be attached when the discs have been hoisted to the summit of the tower. To make a start, the pilot sets the engine going at full speed, and releases a catch which had previously prevented the carriage from moving. The machine darts forward, and in a few yards has attained sufficient speed to lift it from the rail, against which, however, it is kept by depressing the elevators. On reaching the end of the rail it is shot from the carriage, and, the elevators being now quickly raised, rises into the air. Against the wind the machine can be started along the rail by propellers without the aid of the weights.

PAULHAN DOING RECORD FLIGHT ON VOISIN BIPLANE AT RHEIMS.

THE VOISIN BIPLANE

This machine, which came into prominence at the beginning of 1908 as the first successful rival to the Wrights' Flier, is based, as regards its general lines, on the cellular glider devised in 1898 by Mr. Octave Chanute. It consists of two superposed main decks, 33 ft. by 6 ft. 5 ins. (total

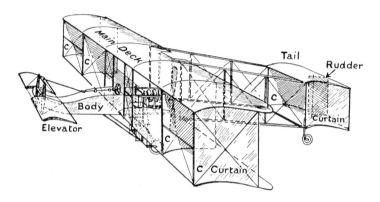

Fig. 2. - DIAGRAM OF VOISIN BIPLANE.

area about 450 sq. ft.) set 5 ft. apart; two smaller superposed decks, 8 ft. by 6½ ft. (total area about 110 sq. ft.), connected to the main decks by a rigid framework, and situated about 13 ft. to the rear to form a tail; an elevator (total area about 50 sq. ft.) mounted 4½ ft. in front of and on a level with the lower main deck on the end of a projecting girder, in which are situated the pilot's seat and the control gear. The "tail" is closed at each side by two vertical curtains, extending about three quarters of the distance from the front of the trailing edge. The purpose of these curtains is to give vertical stability and obviate the need for warping of the decks or the use of balancing planes. A single vertical rudder inside the tail serves for horizontal steering (Fig. 2).

Power is supplied by a 50 horse-power engine geared direct to a single high-speed propeller astern of the main decks. The decks are all curved - the curve depth being one-fifteenth of the fore and aft width of the

deck - and covered on the lower side only of the ribs, which are attached to two main cross-spars. The elevator is double surfaced, its horizontal pivot passing between the two surfaces.

The machine runs on four wheels, two under the main decks and two under the tail. When at rest, the decks make an angle of 8° with the horizontal, and lift at a speed of about 30 miles per hour. When the machine has risen into the air and the speed is increased, this angle diminishes to about 2°.

A very interesting feature of the Voisin aeroplane is the steering control, of which a diagrammatic sketch (Fig. 3) is given. A steering wheel of **VOISIN STEERING CONTROL.** motor-car type operates a horizontal rod, which can be moved backwards and forwards, and also revolved, in sockets on the body. The rod is connected through a universal joint and a second rod to the elevator. On a drum mounted on the steering pillar are wound the wires control-

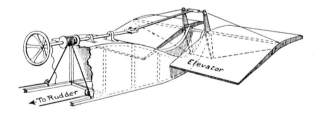

Fig. 3. - DIAGRAM SHOWING STEERING CONTROL OF VOISIN BIPLANE.

ling the vertical rudder in the tail. The driver therefore controls both vertical and horizontal movements of the aeroplane by the same steering wheel. The Voisins claim that the cellular principle is inherently stable, and that it makes for ease of control and safety in descent. The utility of vertical curtains has been questioned. It is maintained in some quarters that they decrease speed and make the machine

TWO VOISIN BIPLANES IN THE AIR TOGETHER AT RHEIMS. *(Photo, Illustrations Bureau.)*

MR. GLEN N. H. CURTISS ON HIS BIPLANE. *(Photo, Illustrations Bureau.)*

This machine is the lightest and swiftest of the biplanes that competed at Rheims.

"unhandy" in rounding corners. The popularity of the type, the quickness with which the novice learns how to handle it, and its undoubted longitudinal stability, are decided points in its favour. Nine Voisin machines, having 540 sq. ft. of supporting surface, and weighing, in flying order, 1,250 lbs., were entered for the Rheims meeting.

down enables the pilot to steer the machine and keep it on an even keel. As our photographs show, the carriage under the main decks has four wheels and two long skates. The latter serve to take the main shock of alighting when the impact is sufficiently great to press the wheels a certain distance upwards on their flexible joints.

A FARMAN BIPLANE.   (Photo, Topical)

Observe the flaps at rear of the decks, used for maintaining lateral balance.

THE FARMAN BIPLANE

This type of machine (Fig. 4), which, driven by its inventor, carried off the Grand Prix for distance at Rheims with a flight of 180 kms. (112 miles), won the prize given for carrying the greatest number of passengers (two), and took second place in the altitude contest, is designed on Voisin lines, but dispenses with vertical curtains. The front elevator is placed somewhat high. To assist steering and lateral stability, the rear ends of the main decks are provided with hinge flaps, which hang down when the aeroplane is at rest, but rise during flight into a horizontal position. Flexing them up or

The weight of a Farman aeroplane is about 1,250 lbs., the area of supporting surface about 475 sq. ft.

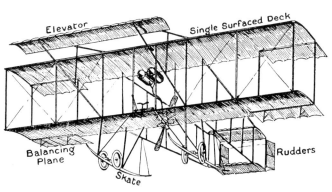

Fig. 4. - DIAGRAM OF FARMAN BIPLANE.

THE CURTISS BIPLANE

This is the smallest of double-decked machines, having but 280 sq. ft. of supporting surface, and weighing only 550 lbs. Yet it won the Gordon Bennett race at Rheims for the fastest flight of 20 kms. (in 15 mins. 50⅗ secs.) and took the first prize for the fastest 30 kms., and the second for the fastest 10 kms. The chief features of this aeroplane - which is of American origin - are two superposed single-surfaced main decks, 28¾ ft. long and 4 ft. 6 ins. wide, 5 ft. apart; a double-decked front elevator (24 sq. ft.); a horizontal tail (12 sq. ft.); a vertical rear rudder; a single propeller, 6 ft. in diameter; and two balancing planes situated between, and partly projecting beyond, the tips of the main decks. The planes are flexed by levers operated by movements of the pilot's body. The elevator and rudder control is practically the same as that used on the Voisin aeroplanes. The decks are covered on the lower surface with rubberised silk, pockets of which enclose the ribs above. An engine of 30 horse-power, weighing, with radiator, about 200 lbs., is used.

The Curtiss is essentially a one-man machine, built for speed rather than for lifting capacity.

THE CODY BIPLANE

At the opposite end of the scale from the Curtiss is the Cody machine, the heaviest and largest aeroplane yet built, and also distinguished as being the first successful flier of British construction. The main decks, double surfaced, 52 ft. long by 7 ft. 6 ins. wide, have an area of 775 sq. ft.; and the front elevators, which also take part of the load, an area of 150 sq. ft. The two vertical rudders are disposed at equal distances fore and aft of the main decks (Fig. 5).

The elevator is in two parts, each of which can be moved independently of the other to serve the purpose of balancing planes. Steering is assisted by warping the decks. Both vertical and horizontal rudders are operated by a single steering wheel immediately in front of the pilot.

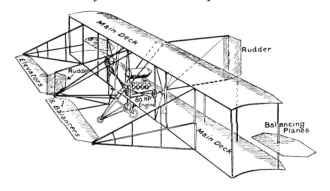

Fig. 5. - DIAGRAM OF THE CODY BIPLANE.

An 80 horse-power "E.N.V." engine drives two propellers mounted between, and near the forward edges of, the main decks. The propellers are peculiar in being wider at the base than at the tips.

So large and heavy is the Cody aeroplane - with pilot it weighs about a ton, or half as much again as the Voisin machine - that the decks have been so designed that two end sections, 16 ft. long each, can be removed. The girder supporting the elevator also is detachable, and the rear rudder frame folds back against the body.

After many unsuccessful attempts, Mr. Cody has at last evolved an efficient machine, capable of great speed. It has flown at nearly 50 miles an hour. On September 8th it put up a record for a cross-country flight by covering over 40 miles in the neighbourhood of Aldershot, not coming to ground until the petrol supply was quite exhausted. At one point an altitude of 600 ft. was attained.

Coming now to the other main class of flying machines, the *Monoplanes*, we may pay attention to three **MONOPLANES.** types - those known as the Blériot, Antoinette and the Esnault-Pelterie. In general appearance they have, when viewed from a distance, a decided resemblance to a bird. Indeed, as shown in some photographs published, the two winged monoplane, with its long trailing tail, might well be mistaken for a gigantic hawk hovering afar off in mid-air.

THE BLÉRIOT MONOPLANE.

The Channel flight has brought into prominence the successful Blériot short-span machine (No. XI), and its less fortunate but considerably larger rival, the Antoinette. The aeroplane on which M. Blériot crossed the "silver streak" is the smallest but one of all the flying machines as regards sustaining surface, for the two wings have a total area

M. BLÉRIOT CROSSING THE BORDEAUX EXPRESS DURING HIS CROSS-COUNTRY FIGHT FROM ETAMPES TO ORLEANS.
(Photo, Topical.)

5 lbs. To obtain the necessary lift a considerable angle of inclination of the decks and high speed are needed. The last factor is attained more easily on a mono-

A BLÉRIOT MONOPLANE IN FULL FLIGHT. *(Photo, Illustrations Bureau)*

of but 150 sq. ft. Since the weight of machine and pilot is over 700 lbs., every square foot of deck has to support nearly

plane by virtue of the absence of the uprights, cross-bracing etc., which form necessary parts of a biplane, and offer

AN ANTOINETTE MONOPLANE IN FLIGHT.

Observe the end shape of the decks.

(Photo, "The Sphere".)

considerable head resistance. We may add that the builders of monoplanes seem to have devoted special attention to the shaping and finish of the decks, which in all cases are covered on both surfaces, and brought to a sharp edge in front.

M. Blériot's small monoplane (Fig. 6) has a span of 28 ft. and a length overall of 25 ft. The decks, which have the rather low

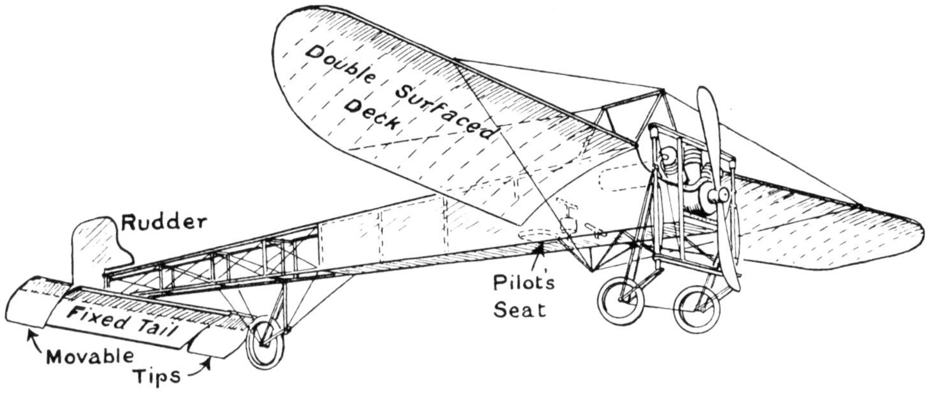

lubricating oil reservoirs are housed between the two surfaces of the wings, and so are completely out of sight; and a 50 horse-power engine is used.

As a class the Blériot monoplanes are very speedy. The Channel was crossed at an

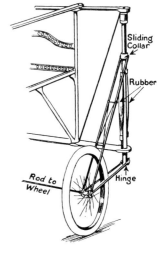

Fig. 7. - WHEELED CARRIAGE OF BLÉRIOT MACHINE.

Fig. 6. - DIAGRAM OF A BLÉRIOT MONOPLANE.

aspect ratio of 4¾ to 1, are rounded at the ends, and are detachable from the body for convenience of transport. The body is a trussed frame about 20 ft. long, tapering to the rear. At the front end is placed the three-cylinder Anzani engine, geared direct to a 6-ft. 6-in. wooden propeller. Immediately behind the engine is the petrol tank, and behind that again the pilot's seat, which is in line with the rear edge of the decks. Near the after end of the body truss, and underneath it, is the fixed tail, with two movable elevating tips. At the extreme end is a vertical rudder. Balancing is effected by warping the main decks. The wheeled carriage, of which a sketch is appended, has some points of interest (Fig. 7).

The No. XII monoplane is a somewhat larger machine, having a deck area of 230 sq. ft. In point of weight it exceeds all other flying machines - except Cody's - with its 1,300 lbs. Nevertheless it has carried two passengers besides the pilot.

In the latest model the petrol tanks and

average velocity of 45 miles per hour. At Rheims, M. Blériot made the fastest time for a single lap of the 10 km. circuit.

THE ANTOINETTE MONOPLANE.

The Antoinette monoplane (Fig. 8) has distinguished itself for its speed and wonderful capacity for attaining great altitudes. During his second attempt to cross the Channel, M. Latham was credited with a velocity of nearly 55 miles per hour. In deck surface and weight, the Antoinette, with its 575 sq. ft. and 1,250 lbs., equals the larger biplanes.

The wings, which have a spread of about 40 ft., project from a boat-shaped body, along the sides of which are set two vertical and one horizontal rudder, besides two fixed vertical stability planes. The decks are inclined at a slight upward angle to each other, and are covered with rubbered silk on both surfaces. To maintain stability, two small wings, or ailerons, are attached to the

LATHAM'S ANTOINETTE AS IT APPEARED FROM
BELOW.   *(Photo, Illustrations Bureau.)*

back of the decks, near their ends.

The vertical steering is effected by a wheel at the pilot's right hand, balancing by a wheel at his left, and horizontal steering by a lever operated by the foot.

The engine is a 50 horse-power Antoinette, driving a single screw 7 ft. 2 ins. in diameter, at 1,100 revolutions per minute. A large skate, projecting in front of the wheeled carriage, helps to absorb the shocks of descent.

At the Rheims meeting the Antoinette monoplane showed to advantage, by winning the Prix d'Altitude, the second and fifth prizes in the Grand Prix distance contest, and the second prize for speed.

THE "R.E.P." MONOPLANE

This monoplane, built by M. Robert Esnault-Pelterie, has decks of 215 sq. ft. area, and weighs about 950 lbs. Its spread is 30 ft. and its length 25 ft. Both decks can be warped to maintain balance. A horizontal movable tail and vertical rudder are placed at the rear end of the body. At the forward end is a 50 horse-power "R.E.P." seven-cylinder air-cooled engine, driving a large four-bladed tractor screw. (This interesting engine is described in the next article.) The body is covered in with fabric to decrease the air resistance.

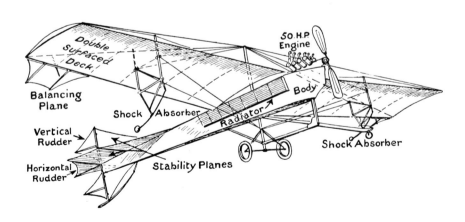

Fig. 8. - DIAGRAM OF ANTOINETTE MONOPLANE.

AERONAUTICAL ENGINES

A review of some of the most interesting of the internal combustion engines that have been designed specially for use on flying machines.

THE provision of sufficient motive power and the reduction of weight to a minimum are two problems which have exercised the constructors of flying machines no less than that of designing efficient supporting surfaces. The Wrights, when they first decided to apply power to their gliders, were confronted by the fact that there was not on the market an engine light enough for their particular purpose. Sir Hiram Maxim had, it is true, lifted his great experimental machine from the ground with the aid of a steam engine which developed a horse-power for every 6 lbs. of avoirdupois, boilers and all fittings included. Professor Langley subsequently propelled a model aerodrome with a steamer that gave an output of 1½ horse-power for its 7 lbs. But the difficulty of keeping these engines supplied with water and fuel, and certain other considerations, had made it evident that another form of prime mover was needed for aerial flight. The development of the internal explosion engine on the motor car prepared the way for the flying machine. Most of the aeronautical engines of today

are, in their general principles, four-cycle motor-car engines greatly improved in the matter of weight, and modified in detail wherever modification makes for lightness. The designer has had in is his favour that aerial engines are not called upon to with-stand the vibrations set up by wheels passing over rough roads, or the strains caused by clutches, gears etc. On the other hand, he has had to be very careful not to cut weight down to danger point, as a failure of any part of the engine may have disas-trous consequences. A very large proportion of aviators' involuntary descents to earth has been due to engine failures; and the same cause was responsible for both of M. Latham's swoops into the Channel. If anything goes wrong with a car engine - which is a rare occurrence nowadays - the driver can stop without risk to investigate. But the aerial motor must be even more *reliable* than the car engine. In addition, it must be extremely *efficient*, for if its power falls below a certain minimum the machine must come down too; and it must be *auto-matic*, supplying itself regularly, and independently of human agency, with fuel, lubricating oil, and electric current.

The parts of an aeronautical engine are necessarily cut as fine as possible in regard to mass. The cylinder walls are reduced to

HOW WEIGHT IS SAVED. the minimum thickness. Valves, pistons, piston-rods, cranks and gearing are made light. To avoid carrying the pound or so of water per horse-power for cooling the engine, air cooling is resorted to widely. Where water is employed, the jackets and radiators are of very thin metal. (At present it seems to be a moot point whether the weight saved by air-cooling is not more than offset by a loss in power.) To increase efficiency the cylinders are often provided with auxiliary exhaust ports, and silencers are omitted.

The need for a fly-wheel of considerable mass on a four-cylinder engine has brought the five, six, seven, eight or more cylinder engine, giving a more or less constant turning effect and perfect balance, into favour, as enabling fly-wheels to be dispensed with.

Automatic lubrication, by means of a force pump, is a *sine qua non*. The aviator's attention and hands are too fully occupied

LUBRICATION. in the maintenance of direction and balance to be available for watching and regulating sight feeds, hand pumps, and gauges. The light mechanical oil pumps now used have been developed to a high pitch of perfection and reliability.

Under the head of carburation some reduction of weight has been effected by replacing the carburettor and large

CARBURATION. induction pipes by a pump delivering unatomized petrol through very small pipes direct to the cylinder. This method is, however, considered to be somewhat wasteful of fuel, and to produce overheating, so that its use is decreasing in favour of the spray carburettor. Magneto and accumulator ignition are used, either separately or in combination.

The aerial motor will doubtless be much improved in the future. Sir Hiram Maxim expects that its weight will be reduced, at no distant date, to 1½ lbs. to the horse-power. Even as at present developed it has shown itself capable of excellent work, despite the fact that, as compared with the car motor, it gives from twice to three times the amount of power per pound weight. It can hardly be doubted that the inventiveness resulting from the necessity for lightness of construction will in due course react upon the motor-car engine, and cause a great reduction in the avoirdupois housed under the "bonnet". One must, nevertheless, not lose sight of the fact that a very light engine of high quality must be an expensive engine, as it requires the best of materials and the most careful manufacture, which last entails highly skilled labour.

We may now review briefly some of the many types of engines which merit notice, paying special attention to distinctive features. In most cases the weight of the engine is given. The figures are, however, hardly a fair criterion for comparison, as some makers include in their totals items which are excluded by others.

FOUR-CYLINDER ENGINES.

In this class the place of honour will be given to the Wright (Fig. 1) type of engine, which, however, has no very striking features. The **THE WRIGHT ENGINE.** four cylinders, arranged in tandem in the usual motor-car fashion, have a bore of 110 mm.* and a stroke of 92 mm. The valves are situated on the top of the head; the inlets are automatic, the exhausts operated by overhead rocking levers. Water cooling is used, water being forced through the four separate water

*For the edification of the reader who is unacquainted with the metric system of measurement, it should be stated that 25 millimetres (mm.) equal one inch.

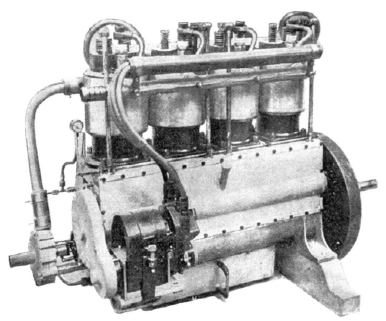

Fig. 1. - THE WRIGHT FOUR-CYLINDER 35 HORSE-POWER ENGINE.
(Photo, Topical.)

British-made aeronautical engines, several interesting points. It is extremely light in proportion to its power. The **THE GREEN ENGINE.**

nominal 35 horse-power type (Fig. 2) scales but 148 lbs. so averaging about 4 lbs. to the horse-power, fly-wheel included; the 60 horse-power model weighs 236 lbs. Lightness has been obtained without sacrificing strength by very careful design. The cylinders and valve ports are cast in high-grade steel, and machined inside and out to the maximum thinness advisable. The water jacket, pressed out of thin copper sheet, encloses completely the upper part of the cylinder and valves. A grooved flange projects from the cylinder to accommodate a rubber ring, against which the slightly bell-mouthed open end of the jacket presses, and so a water-tight joint is obtained. The heat of the engine has no effect on the outer surface of the rubber.

jackets by a pump mounted on the forward end of the crank shaft. Our illustration shows the position of the high tension magneto driven off the cam shaft. On the farther side of the crank-case is a small worm-gear driven pump, which delivers petrol direct into the cylinders, and a pump for forcing lubricating oil from a reservoir in the bottom of the crank-case through the main bearings. A very simple radiator, of flat copper tubes, is mounted vertically on one of the stanchions separating the decks. It is to the credit of the Wrights that they designed and built the first petrol engine ever used for mechanical flight. So far, they have not, apparently, seen any good reason for abandoning the simple type with which they won their first successes.

The Green engine, built for the Green Motor Patents Syndicate by the Aster Engineering Company, has, in addition to the fact that it is one of the at present very few

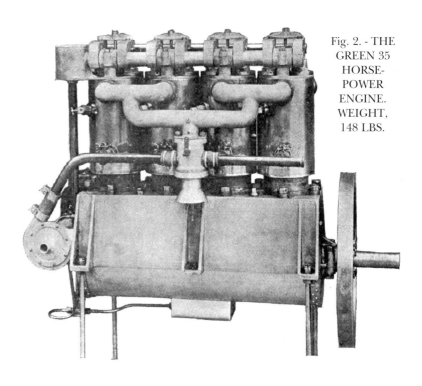

Fig. 2. - THE GREEN 35 HORSE-POWER ENGINE. WEIGHT, 148 LBS.

Fig. 3. - THE GREEN ENGINE, TOP VIEW.
The cam shaft and rocking levers for operating the valves are enclosed in
an oil-tight casing.

Interchangeable valves, in detachable cages, fastened down on the valve ports by internal screwed locking rings, are used. All joints round pipes and ports are made water-tight by pressing the copper jacket against the metal of the cylinder by suitably shaped screwed nipples and washers.

The valve-operating cam shaft runs along the top of the cylinders, and is driven through a vertical spindle (seen on the left) and bevel gear. An oil-retaining casing, which encloses the crank shaft, affords bearings for the eight rocking levers for operating the valves. The casing is divided into two halves vertically, and can be rotated on the shaft when holding-down clamps have been undone, so giving easy access to the valves. (Fig. 3.)

The main bearings are connected directly to the cylinders by vertical bolts passing through columns in the cross divisions of the upper half of the aluminium crank-case. The driving stress is thus taken off the crank-case itself - a very desirable feature. Space is left between the bolts and the columns through

which they pass for conducting lubricating oil from a force pump to the bearings. When the engine is running the only visible point in motion is the fly-wheel.

An 80 horse-power eight-cylinder V type engine comprising the same features was supplied to the War Office for a dirigible balloon.

Our list must include the Anzani three-cylinder engine, as it was one of these that brought M. Blériot safely across the Channel in his memorable flight of July 25th, 1909. The cylinders, of 100 mm. bore and 150 mm. stroke, radiate at angles of 60° from the upper half of the crank-case. The draught from the propeller serves to carry off excess heat, so water-cooling is here dispensed with. The exhaust valves are assisted in scavenging by auxiliary ports in the cylinder walls, uncovered by the piston at the end of the stroke. The engine develops 25 horse-power, and has the merit of being extremely compact.

THE ANZANI ENGINE.

Fig. 4. - THE THREE-CYLINDER 25 HORSE-POWER ANZANI ENGINE, WHICH TOOK M. BLÉRIOT ACROSS THE CHANNEL.

(Photo, Topical.)

Motors of this type are fitted to several Blériot machines. (Fig. 4.)

Fig. 5. - "GNOME" REVOLVING SEVEN-CYLINDER ENGINE ATTACHED TO PROPELLER, WHICH IT CARRIES ROUND WITH IT.

This engine develops 50 h.p., and weighs only 160 lbs. Mr. Henry Farman used a "Gnome" for his record flight of 112 miles at Rheims.

(Photo, Topical.)

We now come to a very interesting class, the five and seven cylinder star-shaped engines, with cylinders radiating at equal distances from the circumference of a central crank-case. The advantage of an odd number of cylinders thus arranged is that it gives explosions at equal distances in continuous sequence. Thus, the firing order of the cylinders of a seven cylinder engine is 1, 3, 5, 7, 2, 4, 6, 1, 3, 5, etc. In the case of six cylinders, arranged in star fashion, there must either be a 1, 2, 3, 4, 5, 6 sequence of explosions during one revolution, and no explosions during the next, or the explosions must occur at irregular intervals: 1, 3, 5, 2, 4, 6, 1, 3, 5 etc.

SEVEN-CYLINDER ENGINES.

A seven-cylinder engine which has proved very successful, and was used on two of the Farman and one of the Voisin machines at the Rheims meeting, is the "Gnome" (Fig. 5). A peculiarity of this engine is that the cylinders and crank-case revolve round a *fixed* crank-shaft, from which the pistons get a push-off. Their rapid motion through the air cools the cylinders sufficiently without the aid of water circulation - which would be difficult to arrange on a rotary engine - and renders a fly-wheel unnecessary. This last feature means a considerable saving of weight. In this engine no aluminium is used, and most of

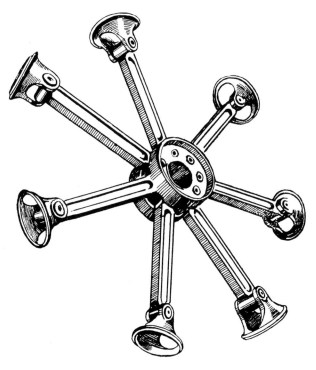

Fig. 6. - THE SEVEN PISTON RODS AND COMMON "BIG-END" OF A "GNOME" ENGINE.

One of the seven rods is integral with the big-end. The other six work on pins passing through it.

the parts are of nickel steel forged by hand.

The stationary and hollow crank-shaft is attached rigidly to the frame of the flying machine, the cylinders and crank-case to the propeller itself - a position which gives the most efficient cooling - or to the propeller shaft. If circumstances demand, the engine can be mounted with its axis vertical, to drive the propeller shaft through bevel gearing.

All seven connecting rods work on a single crank. One of the seven, the "master", carries a double-disc big-end, pierced with six pairs of holes to accommodate the six pins for the rods (see Fig. 6). The big-end itself is separated from the crank by ball bearings.

The 50 horse-power engine, with cylinders of 120 mm. stroke and 110 mm. bore, weighs but 160 lbs., or but little more than 3 lbs. to the horse-power.

Fig. 7. - THE "BAYARD-CLÉMENT" 55 HORSE-POWER SEVEN-CYLINDER ENGINE. WEIGHT, 155 LBS.
The cylinders are stationary, but no fly-wheel is needed.   (*Photo, Topical.*)

The explosive mixture is drawn by the movements of the pistons through the crank-shaft into the crank-case, whence it finds its way into the cylinders through automatic inlet valves situated in the piston heads. These valves are counterbalanced, so as not be be affected by the centrifugal force of rotation; the same remark applies to the exhaust valves on the cylinder heads, operated by rods and rocking levers from cams rotated by epicyclic gearing at the end of the crank-case. The magneto and a pump for circulating lubricating oil are mounted on the shaft, and do not revolve with the engine.

The Bayard-Clément seven-cylinder engine (Fig. 7) differs from the "Gnome" in that the cylinders are stationary and the crank revolves. The exhaust and inlet valves of each cylinder, situated on the head, are operated by a single rocking lever. A small pump, mounted in the crank-case on the crank-shaft, drives water through jackets surrounding the cylinders. The carburettor, outside the case, is connected by a single pipe to a chamber inside the case adjacent to the pump. From this chamber pipes run through the walls of the case to the seven

THE BAYARD-CLÉMENT ENGINE.

inlet valves. At the opposite end of the case is the cam which works all seven valve-tappet rods. The distributor is driven by a half-speed shaft, and the magneto by a cross-shaft and bevel gearing.

The engine is mounted with its shaft vertical, as shown in Fig. 7. A bevel gearing is therefore needed to impart motion to the horizontal propeller shaft. Cylinders, bore 110 mm., stroke 92 mm.; power developed, 55 horse-power; weight, about 155 lbs. No fly-wheel is used, as the explosions, occurring at regular intervals, give the crank a constant torque.

The "R.E.P." (Robert Esnault-Pelterie) the first successful seven-cylinder engine, has all the cylinders mounted on the upper half of the crank-case, four being in one plane and three in another. **THE "R.E.P." ENGINE.** The crank has two throws, operated by four and three pistons respectively, the piston rods of each group being attached to a single big-end. Extremely light pistons are used, and to save weight the bearings for the gudgeon pin of the piston rod are made part of a piece which screws into the socket in the centre of the piston head, and is secured by a screw. A peculiar feature of this engine is that one valve passage serves for both inlet and exhaust. The inlet valve is of the ordinary mushroom-headed type. The exhaust valve has the form of a cylindrical collar surrounding the inlet valve stem, and moving up and down in a cage, the walls of which are perforated. When the collar uncovers the ports, the cylinder is put into communication with the exhaust pipe. The seven-cylinder "R.E.P." weighs 115 lbs., and develops 30 horse-power. A ten-cylinder engine with two sets of five cylinders, mounted in four planes on top of the crank-case, is made. It develops 40 - 50 horse-power. The cylinders of these motors are provided with external fins, and are cooled by air draught.

This section may end with reference to the Adams Farwell five-cylinder revolving air-cooled engine. Like the Bayard-Clément, it runs round a vertical crank-shaft. The 36 horse-power size is remarkably light - only 97 lbs. The 63 horse-power type weighs 4 lbs. per horse-power. Centrifugal force is used instead of the usual coiled springs to close the valves.

EIGHT-CYLINDER ENGINES.

The first extremely light aeroplane engine put on the market was the Antoinette, which has won a high reputation for itself. The air-cooled type scales only about 2½ lbs., the water-cooled about 5 lbs., per horse-power. The **THE ANTOINETTE.** cylinders, of forged steel, are grouped in two sets of four, mounted at right angles to one another on the top of an aluminium crank-case. Two pistons operate each of the four throws of the crank-shaft. The cam-shaft for working the eight exhaust valves is situated inside the case over the crank-shaft. By moving this shaft slightly end-ways the engine can be reversed. The inlet valves are automatic.

Where water cooling is used, a thin copper dome-topped jacket surrounds the cylinder and the guide of the exhaust valve stem. At the bottom the jacket is soldered to an external ring on the cylinder.

Lubricating oil is forced by a small pump into a tube running along the inside of the top of the crank-case, and squirted in all directions through a number of tiny holes on to the crank and cam-shafts, pistons, rods, and cylinder walls. Carburation is produced by a little petrol pump driven by the engine, which delivers petrol into eight little distributors placed near the inlet valves. The distributors store the petrol during the three non-suction strokes. When the inlet valve opens the petrol is drawn into the cylinder, being pulverized and vapourised during the process. The supply is regulated by altering the stroke of the pump's plunger. This system avoids the use of long induction pipes, and saves a few pounds of weight.

Engines of the eight-cylinder V class include that manufactured by the Wolseley

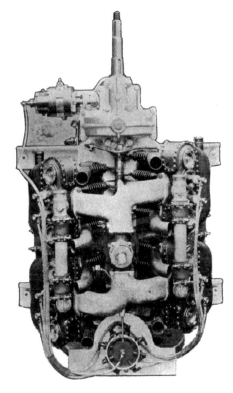

Fig. 8. - THE WOLSELEY EIGHT-CYLINDER 60 HORSE-POWER ENGINE. WEIGHT, 340 LBS.
In this type the propeller is driven off the cam-shaft at half-engine speed.

THE WOLSELEY ENGINE.

Tool and Motor Car Company (Figs. 8 and 9). This firm's engine has cylinders of 3¾-inch bore and 5-inch stroke. All the valves are operated mechanically by a central cam-shaft and rockers. The cylinders, of close-grained cast-iron, are cast in pairs, and each pair is surrounded by a water-jacket shaped out of planished sheet aluminium. Water circulation through the jackets is on the thermo-syphon principle, which does not require a pump.

A float feed and spray type carburettor is mounted in the centre of the engine directly over the cam-shaft - an arrangement which allows of short induction pipes, and ensures an equal distribution of explosive mixture to the cylinders. The weight of the engine, complete with exhaust pipes, is 340 lbs.; the power developed at 1,350 revolutions per minute is 50 B.H.P.; and the maximum obtainable 60 B.H.P. This gives an average of about 6 lbs. per horse-power. For aeroplane work the engine may be arranged to drive the propellers direct from the crank-shaft, or, by means of gearing, at cam-shaft speed. For large propellers the second method is preferable.

The Fiat, Jap, Pipe, and Renault are all air-cooled, but differ considerably in detail. The Fiat (Fig. 10) is enclosed in a circular case, through which a strong current of air is driven by a fan. The combustion heads are detachable for cleaning the inside of the cylin-

OTHER EIGHT-CYLINDER V ENGINES.

ders. The engine develops about 40 horse-power, and weighs 135 lbs.

The English-built Jap engine has a bore of 85 mm., and a stroke of 95 mm., and

Fig. 9. - WOLSELEY ENGINE, DIRECT DRIVE TYPE. END VIEW.

develops 30 - 35 horse-power at 1,000 revolutions per minute, and weighs about 5½

Fig. 10. - "FLAT" EIGHT-CYLINDER 40 HORSE-POWER AIR-COOLED ENGINE. WEIGHT, 135 LBS.

(Photo, Topical.)

lbs. to the horse-power. The 70 horse-power Pipe engine (Fig. 11) weighs 280 lbs., and has cylinders of 100 mm. bore and 100 mm.

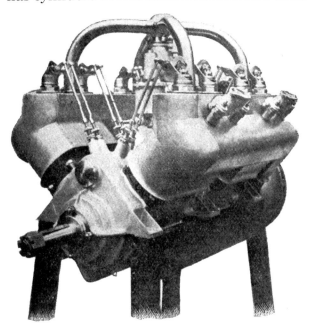

Fig. 11. - EIGHT-CYLINDER 70 HORSE-POWER "PIPE" AIR-COOLED ENGINE. WEIGHT, 280 LBS.
The cylinders are enclosed in jackets, through which air is forced by a fan.

(Photo, Topical.)

stroke. It works at very high speeds - up to 2,000 revolutions per minute. The cylinders, furnished with longitudinal cooling ribs, are covered by light aluminium jackets, through which air is forced by a centrifugal pump mounted on the crankshaft. Another interesting feature is that the valves of each cylinder are concentric, and operated by pairs of overhead rockers, one of which is forked so as to allow the point of the other to move through it.

The Gobron engine (Fig. 12) is very distinctive both externally and internally. The eight cylinders are arranged in four pairs to form a cross. In **THE GOBRON.** each cylinder are two pistons working in opposite directions. When an explosion occurs the pistons are forced apart, one moving towards, the other away from, the crank-shaft. The eight inner pistons have the usual connecting rods to the crank; the outer pistons of a pair of cylinders are connected to a common cross-beam from which long connecting rods run outside the cylinders to separate cranks, set in line at an angle of 180° to the central crank.

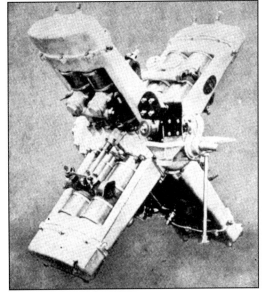

Fig. 12. - EIGHT-CYLINDER CROSS-SHAPED 'GOBRON' ENGINE.
The 80 horse-power type weighs 440 lbs.

(Photo, Topical.)

THE CRANKS AND CRANK-CASE OF ONE OF THE 220 HORSE-POWER ENGINES BUILT FOR "CLÉMENT-BAYARD II".

(Photo, Illustrations Bureau.)

THE CONSTRUCTION OF AEROPLANES AND AERIAL PROPELLERS.

APART from the engine, propeller, and under-carriage, the aeroplane may appear to the uninitiated to be an apparatus that could easily be constructed by any person "clever with his hands". The decks are merely wooden frames covered on one or both sides by fabric, the spars and outriggers nothing but easily-shaped pieces of wood. Such staying with cross wires as is necessary looks a simple enough job. In short, the building of an ordinary pleasure boat would seem to be a much more difficult business for any one who had never tried his hand on it before.

A closer examination of the matter shows, however, that the aeroplane is not so simple a structure as a first view might lead one to think. The designer has constantly to wrestle with an arch enemy, weight, which will sneak its way in if given half a chance; and in keeping it at bay, he must be careful not to open the door to weakness. Then, too, he has to beware of exposing an undue amount of resisting - as distinguished from lifting - surface to the air, lest he should waste the power of his engines in useless work.

To begin with the materials used. Bamboo is commonly considered to be extraordinarily strong for its weight. As a matter of fact, it is in this respect decidedly inferior to many other woods; while its hollowness, and the impossibility of shaping it to any required section, restrict its usefulness considerably. A table of relative strengths shows that Honduras mahogany is, weight for weight, two and a half times as tough as bamboo; lancewood, twice; spruce, one and a half times; ash, one and a third times.

As the chassis of a motor car is built entirely of metal, but different metals are used for different purposes, so in the wooden framework of an aeroplane we find different kinds of wood selected for special duties. Upright stanchions between decks may be of ash; the main spars of spruce; the ribs **WOODS USED.** of ash, hickory, or poplar - woods which can easily be bent to the proper curves. For the main spars of a deck, spruce is most commonly used when it can be obtained in sufficient lengths, and is free from knots and "shakes". To the spars are attached the ribs, which are steamed and bent to shape on wooden templates. The number of spars varies according to the type of machine. Biplane decks usually have two only. A monoplane deck, having to rely on itself for stiffness, as the girder form of construction is not available with a single tier of decks, may possess several auxiliary spars, in addition to the two main ones. These last, in the case of the Blériot short-span monoplane, have projecting ends which fit into sockets in the body of the machine, to

Fig. 1. - A SINGLE-SURFACED DECK, SHOWING POCKETS COVERING SPARS.

render the wings easily detachable for transport.

Decks are either single or double-surfaced. The first type (see Fig. 1) has the ribs attached to the top of the **DECKS.** front spar, and to the under side of the rear spar. The fabric - cotton cloth or silk impregnated with rubber or faced with celluloid - is fastened to the underside of the ribs, and the rear spar and the ribs are

AT WORK IN AN AEROPLANE FACTORY.

enclosed in pockets of the same material, so that no surfaces may be opposed squarely to the passage of the air. This method of construction is economical in fabric, but the attachment of the pockets is a somewhat troublesome business.

For double-surfaced decks (see Fig. 2) the spars, other than the front one, are

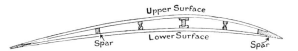

Fig. 2. - A DOUBLE-SURFACED DECK, SHOWING SPARS AND BLOCKS SEPARATING UPPER AND LOWER RIBS.

enclosed by the ribs and fabric. This form of deck gives a better "run" for the air over the upper side, which is much more free from excrescences than the single-surfaced deck, and is therefore more efficient.

The fabric must be stretched as tightly as possible over the framework to prevent undue sagging under pressure of the air. At the trailing edge of the deck it is commonly passed round a taut cable running longitudinally from end to end, or round a fine spar.

The upright stanchions between the decks of a biplane are of oval or fish-shaped sections, and arranged with their greatest diameter fore and aft. These and the decks are braced together diagonally with the piano wires or fine cables drawn tight, and provided with adjustments for taking up any slack. It is important that the wires should not be able to vibrate, since a vibrating wire offers more resistance to the air than one that remains quite taut. The girder formed by the deck spars and the stanchions is, if properly designed, very strong. To test a certain glider, weighing only about 150 lbs., and having a 30-ft. span, the ends of the decks were supported on stools, and a 14-stone passenger took his seat at the centre. The deflection was only half an inch.

Outriggers and the body work of a machine are also built up on the girder principle, so as to be able to withstand sudden and violent strains. A monoplane body is given a more or less **BODYWORK.** decided torpedo or boat shape, tapering somewhat abruptly towards the front and gradually towards the tail, as shown by our illustrations of the Blériot and Antoinette machines. The covering-in of the body with tightly stretched fabric helps to lessen its resistance to the air.

A very important part of an aeroplane is the chassis or wheeled carriage, which supports most of the weight while the machine is at rest, and enables it to run easily over the ground **THE CHASSIS.** when getting up speed for a start. In the chassis steel tubing is employed, as wood could not be relied upon to resist the sudden shocks caused by alighting. Two or more wheels, shod with pneumatic tyres, are generally placed under the main decks, and one or two under the tail where a horizontal tail is fitted. Cody and Curtiss use three in front, Farman four, and Voisin two. Voisin and Blériot mount their wheels castor fashion, so as to adjust themselves automatically to the direction which the aeroplane may take, and interpose springs to minimise shocks to the body of the machine. Special springs are provided to bring the wheels into a fore and aft position when the aeroplane rises from the ground.

The Wrights, by dispensing with a wheeled chassis, reduced the total weight of their biplane and also its air resistance considerably. The Voisin chassis accounts for 250 lbs. or half as much again as the main decks.

SCREW PROPELLERS

Good design of aeroplanes and high engine power in proportion to weight are of little avail, if the means of converting the engine power into work are inefficient.

Locomotives driven over rails and roads are enabled to transmit their force from the moving body to the fixed surface without appreciable loss. But in water and air, which can be displaced easily, the problem of getting, so to speak, a good push-off is one that has demanded close investigation and a huge amount of experiment.

For moving a ship or a flying machine the screw propeller has no rival. The marine

way that the increase of angle may counterbalance the decrease in rotary speed, and enable all parts of the blade's surface to push back the air with an equal velocity. Otherwise, there would be a great waste of power, some portions of the blade acting as a drag on the others.

A propeller blade would, if flattened and set square to the axis of the propeller shaft, offer a minimum turning resistance; if set with its surfaces in line with the shaft, a maximum resistance. In neither case would it have any lift or thrust. The designer has to consider how to curve the blades so as to give a maximum thrust for a minimum windage, which is the counterpart of drift, and at the same time he must be careful to make the surfaces as smooth as possible in order to keep air-friction very low.

CONSTRUCTING A FOUR-BLADED PROPELLER OUT OF
SUPERIMPOSED LAMINAE OF WOOD.

(Photo, London Electrotype Agency.)

propeller has been brought to great perfection; air propellers are being improved rapidly, but are still, as a class, wasteful of power.

The air propeller is in principle closely allied to the curved deck of the aeroplane. As it revolves it strikes the air at an angle, and produces *thrust*, which is the counterpart of the lift of a deck. Owing to the fact that the speed of the parts of a propeller blade vary with their distance from the centre of rotation, it is necessary to increase the steepness of the angle of the blade gradually from the tip to the base in such a

The efficiency of a screw is gauged by the amount of thrust which it gives in proportion to the force exerted to turn it. The thrust itself is arrived at by multiplying the weight of the mass of air acted on in a second by the **THRUST.** velocity in feet per second at which that mass of air is moved. The amount of air engaged varies - the pitch multiplied by the number of revolutions per second.

Assuming that the screw is perfectly efficient, the full thrust for power may be obtained either by using a small screw revolving at engine speed, or a larger screw turning at less than engine speed. In the

A PROPELLER WHIRLING AT HIGH SPEED. *(Photo, Illustrations Bureau.)*

propeller turning at comparatively low speeds gives a greater thrust than a smaller propeller driven at very high speed, the power exerted being the same in both cases, and the pitch proportioned to give the requisite flight speed necessary to support the aeroplane. For this reason the Wrights use two large slow-speed propellers, to which is due, in no small degree, the high efficiency of their machines proportionately to the horse-power of the motors employed. Convenience of attachment is a point in favour of the direct driven propeller, found on most monoplanes and many biplanes. There is a growing tendency, however, to increase the size of the propeller where convenient. We may note, by way of example, that Blériot now uses geared-down screws of large diameter for his heaviest monoplanes.

The highest efficiency obtained so far by an aerial propeller does not exceed probably 70 per cent. It is anticipated that this may be improved upon until 85 to 90 per cent of the engine power is usefully applied. This will make possible a considerable reduction in weight of engine, which in turn will lead to a diminution in the size of aeroplanes.

first case the mass of air is less than in the second case, but the velocity imparted to it is greater; in the second, the mass is larger, but the velocity less. The essential point is to proportion and gear the propeller so that the engine shall be able to run at its most efficient speed.

So far the imparting of motion to air by a fixed propeller has been considered. To obtain the rate of progression in feet per **Slip.** minute at which a machine would be driven by the propeller through the air one must multiply the pitch of the propeller in feet by the number of revolutions per minute, and deduct the "slip" - that is, the velocity of the air flung back by the propeller. A propeller with a 5-foot pitch revolving four hundred times per minute would have a "designed" forward speed of 2,000 feet per minute. If the air left it at 500 ft. per minute, the actual speed of the machine would be 1,500 ft. per minute. High velocity of slip is not necessarily a test of thrust, as it depends largely on the resistance of the machine to the air.

In practice, it is found that a large

Propellers are made of steel, aluminium, magnalium, and various kinds of wood. On the whole, the wooden **CONSTRUCTION** propeller appears to **OF PROPELLERS.** be most satisfactory. It can be made exceedingly light without sacrificing strength, keeps its shape well under heavy pressure, and admits a surface polish which reduces skin friction practically to vanishing point. The woods selected for its manufacture are walnut and spruce. The last is very light, easily shaped and tough.

AVIATION RECORDS.

Date.	Aviator.	Place.	Type of Machine.	Duration of Flight.	Distance, etc.
1897. Oct. 17.	Ader.	Satory, France.	Monoplane.	......	1,000 ft.
1903. Dec. 17.	Orville and Wilbur Wright.	Dayton, U.S.A.	Biplane.	59 secs.	......
1905. Sept. 26.	,,	,,	,,	18 min. 9 sec.	11 miles.
,, 29.	,,	,,	,,	19 min. 55 sec.	12 miles.
Oct. 3.	,,	,,	,,	25 min. 5 sec.	15½ miles.
,, 4.	,,	,,	,,	33 min. 17 sec.	21 miles.
,, 5.	,,	,,	,,	38 min. 3 sec.	24½ miles.
1906. Aug. 22.	A. Santos Dumont.	Bagatelle, France.	,,	Rose from the ground.	First public flight.
Sept. 14.	,,	,,	,,	A few seconds.	......
Oct. 24.	,,	,,	,,	4 sec.	160 ft.
Nov. 13.	,,	,,	,,	7 sec.	270 ft.
,, 13.	,,	,,	,,	21⅕ sec.	722 ft.
1907. Oct. 15.	H. Farman.	Issy, France.	,,	21 sec.	937 ft.
,, 26.	,,	,,	,,	27 sec.	1,267 ft.
,, 26.	,,	,,	,,	31⅗ sec.	1,322 ft.
,, 26.	,,	,,	,,	52⅖ sec.	2,529 ft.
1908. Jan. 13.	,,	,,	,,	1 min. 28 sec.	1,093 yards. (First circular flight.)
Mar. 21.	,,	,,	,,	3 min. 31 sec.	1·24 miles.
April 11.	L. Delagrange.	,,	,,	6 min. 30 sec.	2·43 miles.
May 30.	,,	Rome.	,,	15 min. 26 sec.	7·88 miles.
,, 30.	H. Farman.	Ghent, Belgium.	,,	......	1,360 yards. With E. Archdeacon as passenger; first public passenger flight.
July 6.	,,	Issy, France.	,,	20 min. 19⅗ sec.	12·66 miles.
Sept. 6.	L. Delagrange.	,,	,,	29 min. 53⅘ sec.	14·23 miles.
,, 9.	Orville Wright.	Fort Myer, U.S.A.	,,	57 min. 31 sec.	......
,, 10.	,,	,,	,,	1 hr. 5 min. 52 sec.	......
,, 11.	,,	,,	,,	1 hr. 10 min. 24 sec.	......
,, 12.	,,	,,	,,	1 hr. 14 min. 20 sec.	......
,, 12.	,,	,,	,,	9 min. 6 sec.	With Major Squier; record passenger flight.
,, 21.	Wilbur Wright.	Le Mans, France.	,,	1 hr. 31 min. 25⅘ sec.	41 miles.
,, 25.	,,	,,	,,	11 min. 35 sec.	With passenger.
Oct. 3.	,,	,,	,,	55 min. 37⅘ sec.	,,
,, 6.	,,	,,	,,	1 hr. 4 min. 26⅕ sec.	,,
,, 10.	,,	,,	,,	1 hr. 9 min. 45⅗ sec.	34·2 miles. With passenger.
,, 30.	H. Farman.	Châlons, France.	,,	20 mins.	16·5 miles. First cross-country flight. Châlons to Rheims.
,, 31.	L. Blériot.	Toury, France.	Monoplane.	......	17·5 miles. First cross-crountry flight, with return to starting-point; Toury to Artenay and back; two landings on the way.
Dec. 18.	Wilbur Wright.	Le Mans, France.	Biplane.	1 hr. 54 min. 53⅗ sec.	62 miles.
,, 31.	,,	,,	,,	2 hr. 20 min. 23⅕ sec.	77½ miles.
1909. July 25.	L. Blériot.	Calais to Dover.	Monoplane.	37 min.	30 miles.
Aug. 7.	R. Sommer.	Châlons, France.	Biplane.	2 hr. 27 min. 15 sec.	......
,, 25.	L. Paulhan.	Rheims, France.	,,	2 hr. 43 min. 24⅘ sec.	82 miles.
,, 26.	H. Latham.	,,	Monoplane.	2 hr. 17 min. 21⅗ sec.	96½ miles.
,, 27.	H. Farman.	,,	Biplane.	3 hr. 4 min. 56⅗ sec.	112 miles.
,, 29.	,,	,,	,,	10 min. 39 sec.	6·21 miles. First flight with two passengers.
Sept. 8.	S. F. Cody.	Aldershot.	,,	1 hr. 3 min.	46 miles. First cross-country flight in England.
,, 17.	Orville Wright.	Berlin.	,,	Attained altitude of	607 feet.
,, 18.	,,	,,	,,	1 hr. 35 min. 47 sec.	Record with passenger.
,, 19.	H. Rougier.	Brescia.	,,	Attained altitude of	650 feet.
,, 30.	O. Wright.	Berlin.	,,	Attained altitude of	902 feet.

For Records of Dirigible Balloons see page **64.**

DIRIGIBLE BALLOONS

IN the minds of a good many persons there undoubtedly exists a confusion as regards the terms "airships" and "flying machines". That this should be so is some-

TERMINOLOGY. what curious, as a little thought must make it evident that a "ship" implies something that floats by virtue of its own buoyancy in the medium through which it moves; and the term airship, therefore, must apply only to the dirigible balloon. On the other hand, every living thing that *flies* is heavier than air, and supports itself only by the action of moving parts on the air. Hence the words "flying machine" obviously refer to contrivances which lift as well as propel themselves by the development of power. The airship has its counterpart in the submarine boat; the flying machine may be compared to the hydroplane, which is supported when moving at high speed by the resistance to water of more or less oblique horizontal surfaces, and not by buoyancy.

If the atmosphere surrounding our globe were untroubled by currents, the dirigible balloon would have "arrived" many years ago. To make a cigar-shaped envelope, attach thereto a car, and provide motive power of some kind would not have presented very serious difficulties; and the improvement of motors would have greatly increased the, at first, unavoidably low speeds. Unfortunately, from the point of view of the "dirigible", the air ocean has a constant motion, at times almost imperceptible, at others terrifying in its velocity. Even the more gentle of the intermediate strengths of current have to be reckoned with.

The resistance of the air to a large body moving through it demands that the shape of a dirigible should be considered carefully. A sphere has greater volume than a body of any other shape proportionately to its surface. **SHAPE OF AIRSHIPS.** But to drive a sphere through the atmosphere requires half the power needed to propel a circular plane of equal diameter flatways on; and therefore a spherical form is evidently not suited for a "dirigible". On the other hand, the more or less cigar-shaped form adopted, though offering less resistance, has an envelope that is heavy relatively to the volume of gas imprisoned. Its efficiency is, however, augmented by a general increase in dimensions - the proportions being constant - as the doubling of surface area of the envelope far more than doubles the cubical contents.

To consider for a moment the shape. Experiment has shown that a hemispherical prow and a conical tail give the best results

THE "COLONEL RENARD" AT RHEIMS. *(Photo, Illustrations Bureau.)*

This is one of the smaller French non-rigid dirigibles, with stabilising ballonets at the stern.

THE MALÉCOT SEMI-RIGID AIRSHIP.   *(Phote, Bolak.)*

To the balloon are attached a number of planes, which can be set at an angle to the horizontal to give vertical motion.
In case of the collapse of the gas-holder, they would also have some of the effect of a parachute.

as regards minimising resistance. It is much less important to avoid a blunt prow than to keep the lines of the after-part fine, since the resistance of the air to being pushed aside is small as compared with the "suck" of a badly-shaped stern. The ideal form has been adopted for a recently built Italian airship, and, with modification, for most other dirigibles. German examples - the Zeppelins excluded - have the hemispherical prow and conical tail, but these are separated by a cylindrical body. Some French airships have a conical prow. The Zeppelins are distinguished by a very long cylindrical body, terminated at both ends by what may be termed a spherical cone. In this type the head resistance is said to be about one-fifth of that of a circular plane of the same area as the cross-section of the body. In practice, the shape of the envelope is governed by several factors other than that of mere resistance, and is more or less of a compromise. In a paper on military aeronautics, Major G.O. Squier, of the United States Army Signal Corps, laid it down that the power consumed in propelling a displacement vessel supported by air or water at any constant speed is considered as being two-thirds consumed by skin-resistance or surface resistance, and one-third by head resistance; and that a dirigible balloon carrying the same weight, other things being equal, may be made to travel about twice as fast as a boat for the same power, or to be made to travel at the same speed with the expenditure of about one-eighth of the

PROWS AND STERNS.

RESISTANCES.

power. "As there are practically always currents in the air reaching at times a velocity of many miles per hour, a dirigible balloon should be constructed with sufficient power to be able to travel at a speed of about 50 miles per hour, in order that it may be available under practical conditions of weather. In other words, it should have substantially as much power as would drive a boat, carrying the same weight, 25 miles an hour, or should have the same ratio of power to size as the *Lusitania*."

The pressure on the envelope of a balloon, when the latter is moving at high velocity relatively to the air, must indent it and cause great increase of resistance unless the envelope be either kept taut by inflation or supported by a rigid framework of some kind. As high **PRESSURE ON THE ENVELOPE.** inflation is prevented by the comparative weakness of the fabric, and even, if feasible, would mean a sufficient compression of the gas to cause a serious loss of buoyancy, the "rigid" school, whose great exponent is, of course, Count von Zeppelin, makes use of an internal skeleton, a light polygonal girder running from stem to stern. The weight of the girder makes great volume necessary, and to obtain this without increasing the head resistance unduly, the body is given a length of rather more than ten diameters. A single container of this shape would be subjected to dangerous surgings of **ZEPPELIN PRINCIPLE.** gas to and fro as either end rose and fell, so Zeppelin has adopted a number of small balloons separated from one another by partitions, and from the changes in temperature of the atmosphere. This subdivision has the further advantage of localising damage to the balloon. Had the ill-fated *République* not had a single chamber, she might have come to ground without fatal results. For non-rigid dirigibles one or more internal air ballonets are used. Air is pumped constantly into them, escaping

again through a valve if the pressure rises above a certain point. The gas chamber also is provided with a valve, act- **BALLONETS.** ing at somewhat higher pressure, so that under no conditions can the distension of the ballonets cause a loss of gas. If the gas is expanded by a rise in temperature, the ballonet is squeezed until the pressure is normal. If, on the other hand, the gas contracts or leaks, the ballonet swells out until equilibrium is restored.

The distribution of the load over the gas holder in such a way as not to strain any part unduly is, in the case of a Zeppelin airship, simplified by the employment of a girder keel. Unless the **DISTRIBUTION OF THE LOAD.** distribution is made properly over a non-rigid envelope, there must be a danger of the balloon collapsing. To simplify the problem a keel or frame fitting the lower side of the envelope is used, and from it are slung the car, motor etc. Dirigibles thus provided are known as semi-rigid, and have some of the stiffness of the Zeppelin type, while being capable of deflation like the non-rigid type, though less convenient for transport by land. The German *Gross* and the French *Lebaudy* and *République* belong to this class.

The rigid airship has a further advantage over the non-rigid in that the propellers can be attached to the gas-holder frame and deliver their thrust at the same elevation as that of the centre of air pressure. In the case of a **APPLICATION OF POWER.** non-rigid airship, the propellers are mounted far below the centre of pressure, and this produced a tilting action and less efficient drive.

Renard, during his experiments in 1884 and 1885, found that his airship began to pitch - tilt up and down longitudinally - as soon as it attained a certain speed. To obviate this tendency, he attached horizontal, fin-like planes to the tail, a practice

 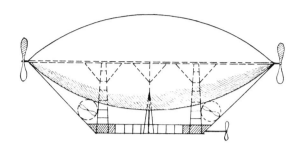

SEVERO'S DIRIGIBLE BALLOON (1902).
The propeller shaft was mounted at the axis of the balloon to give a direct thrust. Two small propellers at the ends of the car were used for lateral steering; a single propeller at the stern for vertical steering.

is, in fact, not a true "ship", as it does not float by its own buoyancy. For lateral steering one or more vertical rudders placed near the stern are used.

DEVELOPMENT OF THE AIRSHIP.

which has been followed in more recent designs. The French *Ville de Paris* and *Clément-Bayard* have, instead of planes, small ballonets, cylindrical in the first case, pear-shaped in the second. (See the illustrations on pages 58 and 57 respectively.) Pitching arises from irregularities in pressure and the presence of ascending or descending air currents, from the leakage of gas, and the shifting of the dead or the live load. The lower the centre of gravity is kept the less will the pitching be. Movable weights for correcting the trim are used. On the Gross airship two ballonets - one forward and the other aft - are connected by a pipe through which air is transferred from one to the other to alter the buoyancy of either end. As Moedebeck remarks in his *Handbook of Aeronautics*, the maintenance of stability in long airships is one of the most difficult problems for the constructor.

STABILITY.

Vertical steering is effected by the aid of planes attached to the balloon or the body, and by altering the longitudinal trim. The Zeppelin airships carry sets of planes fore and aft, which, if set at an angle of 15° to the horizontal, will at 31 miles an hour give a lifting force of nearly a ton, and enable a rapid ascent to be made without throwing away ballast.

STEERING.

The French *Malécot* (see page 47) has, under the envelope, a number of aeroplanes, upon which devolves part of the duty of raising the airship from the ground and keeping it aloft. This particular airship

The first airship to attain an independent velocity was that built by Henry Giffard, the inventor of the famous water injector now commonly used for steam boilers, in 1852. (Fig. 1.) It was about 136 ft. long and 37 ft. in diameter, and had a capacity of 2,000 cubic metres. Its weight was 2,794 lbs. - a striking contrast to the light but extremely powerful petrol engine of today. The car, containing the engine, was suspended from a horizontal rod to which the cordage of the envelope was attached. On September 24th, Giffard made an ascent at Paris, and succeeded in obtaining a speed estimated variously at 4½ and 6¾ miles an hour.

GIFFARD'S DIRIGIBLE.

During the siege of Paris (1870) Dupuy de Lôme built for the French Government a dirigible shaped somewhat similarly to that of Giffard. In place of an engine the muscles

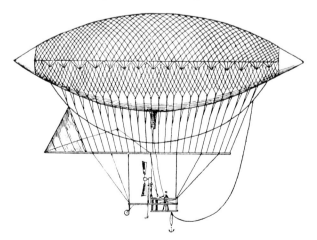

Fig. 1. - GIFFARD'S DIRIGIBLE (1852).
It was propelled by a three horse-power steam-engine, and attained a speed of about six miles and hour.

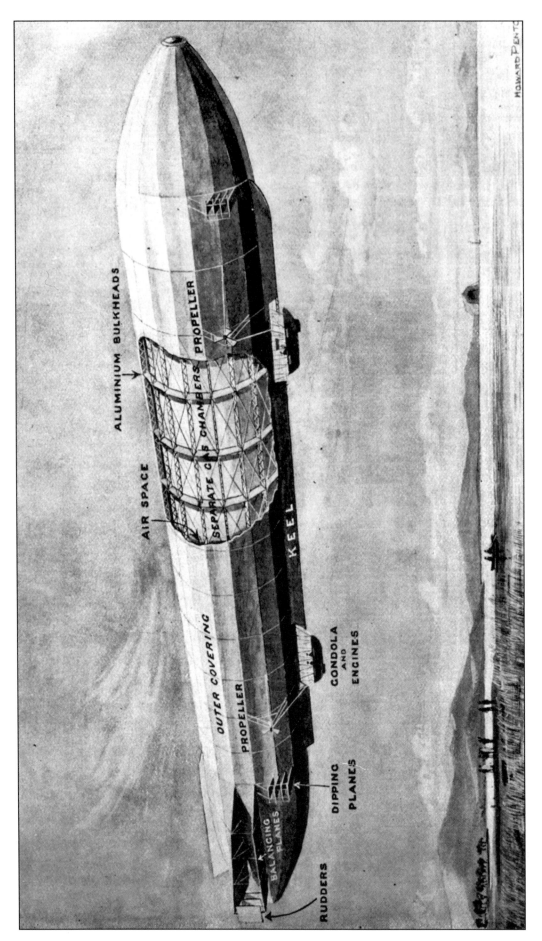

VIEW OF ZEPPELIN DIRIGIBLE, WITH PART OF EXTERNAL COVERING REMOVED TO SHOW THE SEPARATE GAS
CHAMBERS AND LATTICE GIRDERS OF THE FRAME.

The latest patterns have seventeen chambers, and measure 453 feet from bow to stern. Their volume is 15,000 cubic metres.

of eight men were employed to turn a large screw, nearly 30 ft. in diameter, about

DUPUY DE LÔME. twenty-eight times per minute. The airship moved itself at a low speed, but apparently the inventor and the Government did not consider its behaviour sufficiently satisfactory to justify sending it over the beleaguering German army.

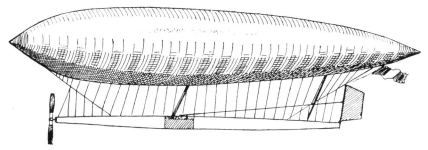

Fig. 2. - RENARD AND KREBS' AIRSHIP (1884).
The first really successful navigable balloon. Propelled by electric motors. It made several considerable voyages at a good speed. Highest velocity attained, about fourteen miles an hour.

Passing over the experiments of Haenlein and Tissandier, we come to the famous airship constructed by Captains

RENARD AND KREBS' DIRIGIBLE. Renard and Krebs of the French army in 1884 and 1885. This balloon (Fig. 2) was of more scientific design than its predecessors, having its largest diameter near the prow, and tapering gradually aft. The volume was comparatively small, only 1,864 cubic meters. As motive power the inventors selected electricity, stored in battery of thirty-two cells of special construction, and used in an 8.5 horse-power motor, which revolved a 23 ft. propeller thirty to forty times per minute. Several successful trials were carried out in August, September, and November 1884, and in August and

SUCCESSFUL TRIALS. September of the following year, the highest speed attained being 14 miles an hour. The dirigible overcame winds of considerable strength, and on five of the seven trials returned to its starting point. It is somewhat strange that the Government

did not continue experiments with so efficient an airship, which, in the words of Renard, had "furnished the first proof of the possibility of manoeuvring a spindle-shaped balloon in the air ocean by means analogous to those which allow ships to perform evolutions in the ocean of water".

During the years 1898 to 1905 the young Brazilian, Alberto Santos Dumont, designed a series of dirigibles. Henri Deutsch, a wealthy member of the French Aero Club, offered in 1900 a prize of £4,000 to any one who should start from the Aero Club park near **SANTOS DUMONT.** Longchamps, sail to and round the Eiffel Tower, and return to the starting point - a distance of about seven miles - in less than half an hour. After several unsuccessful attempts to capture the prize, M. Santos Dumont succeeded, on October 19th, 1901, in covering the stipulated course in a minute less than the limit. The airship used, his No. VI, had a gas bag 33 metres long and 6 metres in diameter, with a volume of 630 cubic metres. An internal air **THE DEUTSCH PRIZE WON.** ballonet, fed by a pump, maintained the tautness of the envelope. From the bag was suspended a long truss carrying a basket-work car for the aeronaut, a 16 horse-power Buchet four-cylinder motor, and at the rear end a propeller four metres long, made of silk stretched tightly over a rigid frame. Steering was effected by a vertical rudder operated from a wheel at the front of the car. Santos Dumont's balloons, though not a great advance on that of Renard and Krebs, proved the suitability of the petrol motor for driving airships, and did a great deal towards stimulating public interest in the possibilities of the dirigible.

Simultaneously with Santos Dumont's

STERN VIEW OF 'ZEPPELIN II' (ORIGINALLY NO. III) LEAVING THE HUGE FLOATING BALLOON SHED
AT FRIEDRICHSHAFEN.
Observe the stability planes at the side, the vertical steering rudders between them, and the elevating planes near the keel.
(Photo, Topical.)

experiments at Paris, Count F. von Zeppelin had been busy at Friedrichshafen, on

COUNT ZEPPELIN'S AIRSHIPS.
Lake Constance, with the construction of a monster dirigible, which is known as *Zeppelin I.* The envelope was 426 ft. long and 37 ft. in diameter, its section being that of a twenty-four sided prism. The framework was built of aluminium alloy, and divided into seventeen small balloons used to give buoyancy. The space between the balloons and the outer

ZEPPELIN I.
covering of pegamoid was ventilated by a constant current of air passed through. The volume of the gas chambers totalled 11,300 cubic metres; the weight, including petrol for a ten hours' flight, cooling water for the engines, and a crew of five men, ten tons. In the long keel attached to the under-side of

the framework were placed two cars, situated about half-way between the centre and the ends, each carrying a 14.7 Daimler petrol motor. Zeppelin adopted two independent motors, so that, if one should fail, the other would be available for manoeuvring the ship and bringing it to earth, if need be. Each motor drove a pair of four-bladed propellers, about 4 feet in diameter, at the very high speed of 1,100 revolutions per minute, through bevel gearing. Reversing gear was included, so that the ship could be moved astern if occasion arose. An installation of electric bells, telegraphs, and speaking tubes assisted the operations of steering.

On July 2nd, 1900, at 7.30 p.m. the first trial was made. At the signal all ropes were released, and the airship rose and moved against the wind, turning now to the left, now to the right, in answer to the movements of the helm. Unfortunately one of the

FIRST TRIALS. rudder cables broke, and Zeppelin decided to descend, which he managed to effect without accident. Further trials took place on October 17th and 21st. During the first of these the airship remained aloft for eighty minutes; during the second, it attained an independent velocity of twenty miles an hour, which quite eclipsed the performance of Renard's *La France*. The tests served to show that, within the limits of its speed, the huge structure could be driven against the wind, and made to circle; also that the design of the framework needed modification to give greater stiffness.

The expense of his experiments had exhausted Zeppelin's finances, and compelled him to appeal to the public for the means with which to continue his researches. But times were bad, and popular interest in aeronautics was as yet unawakened. So four years passed before he had collected sufficient money to construct

ZEPPELIN II. *Zeppelin II*. This airship had a somewhat larger volume than its predecessor, but was much better engined, two 90 horse-power Mercedes motors taking the place of the two 14.7 horse-power Daimlers. Also, the workmanship and design showed a decided advance. For ascensional purposes, two vertical screws, each giving a lift of 240 lbs., were provided.

The trials, made early in 1906, showed that the new craft was much faster than *Zeppelin I*, but that it lacked longitudinal stability. On the last trip the steering gear and the motors failed to act, the airship began to drift before the wind, and a

A DISASTER. descent had to be made into a meadow. During the night, however, a gale arose, drove the airship against a tree, and in a few minutes had reduced it to a complete wreck.

Count von Zeppelin announced his intention to retire from the field after this disaster, but was persuaded by the Government to persist. Within nine months he had *Zeppelin III* afloat. This had nearly 4,000 cubic meters more volume than No. II, being of larger diame-

ZEPPELIN III. ter and length. Two 110 horse-power motors supplied the driving power, the balloon itself had sixteen sides only, instead of the twenty-four sides used previously, as the reduction of number facilitated construction.

On trial the *Zeppelin III* proved a great success, carrying eleven passengers sixty-nine miles in 2 hours 17 minutes, at an average speed of 35 miles an hour. The Government now came forward with the offer to purchase an airship for £100,000 if it could make a continuous flight of twenty-four hours, and land safely. Accordingly, Zeppelin busied himself with the construction of No. IV, wherewith

ZEPPELIN IV. to fulfil the conditions laid down. This ship was ready by the beginning of June 1908. On July 1st she left Friedrichshafen, and travelled westwards along the north shore of Lake Constance towards Schaffhausen. Just before reaching this town she turned southwards and made for town and lake of Lucerne, round which she passed without difficulty. Thence the course was set northwards to Zürich, and, after that city had been passed, eastwards over the Sulgen and Romanshorn to the east end of Lake Constance, and so back to the great floating shed at Friedrichshafen. A distance of 236 miles had been covered in twelve hours - an average

A TRIP OVER SWITZERLAND. of 18⅓ miles an hour - without mishap of any kind. The world was electrified by a performance which threw completely into the shade all previous achievements of dirigibles.

On Tuesday, August 4th, 1908, Zeppelin set out on his first attempt to win the Government subsidy with a twenty-four

"ZEPPELIN IV." ROUNDING STRASSBURG CATHEDRAL SPIRE DURING THE VOYAGE WHICH ENDED IN HER TOTAL DESTRUCTION AT ECHTERDINGEN.

(Photo, Scherl.)

hours' flight. Following the course of the Rhine, the airship passed Basle, Mülhausen, Strassburg, Mannheim, and

A FINE VOYAGE ENDS IN DISASTER. reached Mainz, after a voyage lasting 16 hours 40 minutes. After a descent to make some trifling repairs, the homeward journey began, The great envelope had, however, developed leaks, which, coupled with irregular working of the motors, compelled the count to descend at Echterdingen, near Stuttgart. While the balloons were being inflated, a squall struck the ship, and bumped it violently against the ground. Some petrol ignited, and in a moment the conflagration had reached the highly inflammable hydrogen in the balloons. A few minutes sufficed to destroy the work of months.

This heavy misfortune, coming on the top of a great triumph, roused the patriotism of Germany in a manner that may serve as an object lesson to other nations. Within a few weeks £300,000 were subscribed to enable the aged Count to build yet more Zeppelins for the use of his countrymen.

Zeppelin III was taken in hand, increased as to its length and carrying power by the addition of one more balloon, renamed *Zeppelin II*, and after some very successful tests, taken to Metz to form a unit in the aerial fleet that now has its headquarters on the frontier.

Zeppelin II (new style) is the same size as No. IV, and has to its credit the longest of all airship voyages. On May 29th, at 9.42

A RECORD JOURNEY OF OVER 600 MILES. p.m., it left Friedrichsafen, and took an almost direct line for Berlin, 360 miles distant. The huge dirigible passed over Ulm, Nuremberg, Bayreuth, Plauen, and Leipzig. At the last-named place Zeppelin threw over a telegram addressed to the emperor, expressing his hopes that he might be able to reach Berlin, only 125 miles away, that

day. The news spread through Berlin like wildfire; the whole population turned out to welcome the Count. But a northerly breeze arose and developed steadily into so high a wind that Zeppelin, on reaching Bitterfeld, decided to turn the airship about and run southwards. Late in the evening, the inhabitants of Halle and Weimar saw Zeppelin II pass overhead. By 4.45 next morning she reached Würzburg. Five hours later she was circling the spire of Stuttgart Cathedral. The ship then proceeded to Kirchheim, where the petrol supply began to show signs of exhaustion. At Göppingen a descent was decided upon. During an attempt to land, the airship was driven violently against a tree, which smashed in her bows and held her prisoner, her stern floating well above the ground. Thus ended a

COLLISION WITH A TREE.

38-hour journey, during which well over 600 miles - some calculations make the figures 950, but this is probably excessive - had been covered. Even the records of *Zeppelin IV* had "gone by the board". Though this remarkable achievement also ended in disaster, after temporary repair the airship was able to make its way, with but one rudder running, to Friedrichshafen, where, in the course of a few weeks, it was put into good running order again.

The latest of the Zeppelins, No. III, has three motors of 150 horse-power each, but has not, up to the time of writing, performed any sensational feat. In general features the Zeppelin type has not undergone much alteration. Power, volume, and lifting capacity have been increased, the steering apparatus has been improved, and great accommodation for the crew provided. The rigid, subdivided gas-holder is retained, despite the criticisms of the non-rigid school. Count von Zeppelin has boundless faith in his own invention. So far from being discouraged by the mishaps which must be expected to occur while the lessons of aeronautics are being learned, he

THE FRENCH DIRIGIBLE 'ZODIAC III.'   *(Photo, Topical.)*
The pipe and pump for keeping the internal air-ballonet inflated are noticeable features. Elevated planes mounted on
front of the car. Rudder attached to under-side of the balloon. Non-rigid type.

has propounded a scheme for running regular airship services, as a commercial venture, between Berlin and Copenhagen, Stettin, Bremen, Cologne, Stuttgart, and other important centres, besides pleasure trips down the Rhine into Switzerland.

FRENCH DIRIGIBLES.

The *Lebaudy* airship, built by Julliot and Surcouf in 1902, is of the semi-rigid type, with a keel-shaped floor made of steel tubes. Length, 56.5 metres; greatest diameter, 9.8 metres; volume, 2,784 cubic metres. The car is slung from the floor by steel rods. A 40 horse-power motor operates two screws, one on either side of the car, each 9 feet in diameter. With the engine running at 1,050 revolutions a minute, the thrust of the propellers totals 350 lbs. In 1902, 1903 and 1905, the *Lebaudy* made many successful trips, ranging up to nearly 100 kilometres. The airship behaved so satisfactorily - especially

THE *LEBAUDY* AIRSHIP.

after certain alterations and improvements had been carried out - that it was finally adopted for the French army, and is still in commission.

Two other dirigibles, *La Patrie* and *La République*, were subsequently constructed on Lebaudy lines. The *Patrie* delighted the Parisians in 1907 by a number of evolutions over the capital, and at the end of November made a memorable voyage of 230 kilometres from Paris to Verdun, near the German frontier. Only 140 out of the 190 litres of petrol, and but a small part of the ballast, were used, so that the journey could have been extended for many miles. During part of the trip the elevation was about 3,000 feet. (A few days before the start the *Patrie* had proved her ability to rise 1,300 metres, or 4,300 feet, the record at that time for dirigibles.) Shortly after arriving at Verdun, the *Patrie* was overtaken by a gale while at anchor. A large body of soldiers detached to hold her down kept her captive

THE *PATRIE* AND *RÉPUBLIQUE*.

for some hours. Then she broke away and was swept into the clouds, travelling north-westwards at a high speed. Probably she passed over England and Ireland, and fell into the Atlantic Ocean.

Some details of this airship will be of interest. Length, 197 feet; maximum diameter, 33¾ feet; volume 111,250 cubic feet; stern provided with an **DETAILS OF THE *PATRIE*.** *empennage* (or feathering, like that of an arrow) of two vertical and two horizontal planes, to maintain stability; ballonet, having capacity of one-fifth of the total volume, divided into three compartments by perforated partitions to prevent surging of the air to and fro; boat-shaped car, 16 by 5 by 2½ feet, attached by triangulated steel cables to the rigid frame under the gas-bag, the two last being held together by a net; frame easily released from net, and taken to pieces for transport; car furnished with pyramidal sub-structure to take the shock of landing. A motor of 70 horse-power drove two steel propellers, 8½ feet in diameter, and mounted on each side of the car, at 1,000 or more revolutions per minute. The frame carried vertical and horizontal stabilising planes and a vertical rudder, and a movable horizontal plane was fixed above the car to cause ascent and descent without loss of gas or ballast.

The *République* was very similar to the *Patrie*. It had 2,000 cubic feet more volume, but a somewhat less powerful motor. It **THE *RÉPUBLIQUE*.** made some very good flights, and took part in the French army manoeuvres of 1909. While returning from these to Chalais Meudon, she was destroyed by a propeller blade coming adrift and splitting the balloon. The airship fell 700 feet, and her crew of four men were killed instantaneously.

La Ville de Paris belongs to the non-rigid class. Built in 1906 by Surcouf; length, 200 feet; maximum diameter 34½ feet; volume, 3,200 cubic metres. The ballonet is

THE 'CLEMENT-BAYARD I.' ENTERING ITS SHED. *(Photo, Topical.)*

Observe the great stabilizing ballonets at the stern.

FRENCH NON-RIGID AIRSHIP 'VILLE DE PARIS'. LARGE TRACTOR SCREW IN FRONT.
Length, 62 metres; greatest diameter, 10.5 metres; volume, 3,200 cubic metres; horse-power of motor, 70.
(Photo, Topical.)

divided fore and aft into three compartments by curtains of permeable cloth, not fixed at the bottom, so that when the ballonet is distended air can pass easily from one compartment to another. The car is very long and heavy, and is attached to the gas-bag by a number of ropes running to canvas bands sewn to the side of the bag. This "long" suspension gives a good distribution of weight. A single propeller of large diameter is mounted at the front of the car, and driven by a 75 horse-power motor at 980 revolutions per minute. The distinguishing feature of the *Ville de Paris* is the eight small cylinders, arranged in groups of two, which take the place of the vertical and horizontal stability planes of the *Patrie*. Their weight is exactly equal to the buoyancy of the gas which they contain, so that they have no ascensional effect. They are said to serve their purpose

THE *VILLE DE PARIS*.

very well, but, in spite of their conical forward ends, cause a drag which militates against high speed.

The *Clément-Bayard I*, designed by M. A. Clément, the founder of the famous French motor-car firm, was completed in 1908. Length, 56.25 metres; maximum diameter, 10.58 metres; volume 3,500 cubic metres. The bag has at the tail four large pear-shaped gas ballonets, which communicate with the main bag through holes pierced in the envelope. The air ballonet is unusually large, and has a volume of 1,100 cubic metres. The car is built of steel tubes, and covered with cloth and aluminium sheeting. The vertical rudder has two parallel planes of steel; the horizontal rudder three superposed planes, with a total surface of 16 square metres, and is set slightly forward of the centre of gravity. Both rudders are balanced and

CLEMENT-BAYARD I.

operated through steel cables by irreversible tillers. To diminish vibration, and to enable the instruments in the car to be read more easily, the engine is mounted on a system of springs.

The *Ville de Bordeaux* and *Colonel Renard* have the same general features as the *Clément-Bayard I*. The *Clément-Bayard II*, built for trial in **CLEMENT-BAYARD II.** England, is the largest of all non-rigid airships. It measures 300 feet from stem to stern, and has a volume of 6,300 cubic metres. The bag has a blunt nose and a long conical body and tail. In place of the stabilising ballonets of *Clément-Bayard I*, she carries a vertical plane under the tail. Close to this is the vertical rudder for lateral steering. To distribute the weight of the engines, passengers etc., a car 140 feet long is slung from the gas chamber. About one third of it is available for the engines and living freight.

The *Clément-Bayard II* is engined with two 220 horse-power motors set amidships to drive a couple of two-bladed wooden propellers, 20 feet in diameter, mounted on either side of the car, and revolving in opposite directions. The lifting power of the airship is sufficient to raise twenty-five passengers and enough petrol for a six or seven hundred-mile journey. It is expected that a speed of at least 35 miles an hour will be attained. This airship will be the great rival of the Zeppelins; her carrying power, speed, and radius of action should prove as great, and she may show herself superior as regards alighting and manoeuvring.

In Germany it is recognised that, though the Zeppelin type may have decided advantages for long trips, smaller dirigibles with collapsible gas chambers are more suitable for military purposes. The first non-rigid German dirigible, *Parseval I*, appeared in 1906. It had a hemispherical

GERMAN NON-RIGID 'PARSEVAL II.' FLYING OVER THE TEGELER GROUNDS. *(Photo, Topical.)*

Note the hemispherical prow and conical stern. This balloon has two internal ballonets, and a pump for transferring air from one to the other to regulate the longitudinal trim. Length, 58 metres; greatest diameter, 9.5 metres; volume, 3,800 metres; horse-power of motor, 114.

TAKING OBSERVATIONS FROM A MILITARY DIRIGIBLE BALLOON.

prow and a conical stern. Two air ballonets are used, one at each end, to control the lon-

THE PARSEVAL. gitudinal trim of the gas chamber. For ascending, the rear ballonet is filled and the front ballonet emptied, throwing the centre of gravity of the gas forward, and causing

stiffened by centrifugal force when revolving. Weight is reduced considerably by this system of blading. Larger and more efficient Parsevals were built in 1908 and the present year. *Parseval II* is 58 metres long, has a volume of 3,800 cubic metres, and carries a 114 horse-power engine.

'GROSS II.,' THE GERMAN SEMI-RIGID MILITARY AIRSHIP, IN FLIGHT.   *(Photo, Topical.)*
In general outline it closely resembles the Parseval, but is distinguished by the girder keel from which the car is suspended. This ship was used during the German army manoeuvres of September.

the prow to rise and give the under surface of the bag somewhat of an aeroplane effect. For descending, the process is reversed.

Two other interesting points are the car suspension and the propeller. The car has two pulley wheels on each side at the floor level, round which pass steel cables to the ropes distributing the weight over the whole length of the gas-bag. This arrangement allows the car to adjust its position in accordance with variations of the screw thrust and air pressure. The propeller has four blades of cloth weighted with lead. When at rest the blades hang limp, but are

The *Gross I,* launched in 1907, is a semi-rigid dirigible, with spherical prow and stern. The latest Gross has a volume of 5,000 cubic metres, and includes two air ballonets. The two 3-bladed propellers revolve in the same direc- **THE GROSS AIRSHIPS.** tion. At the rear, horizontal planes are used for stability. We may note that the inventor, Von Gross, has abandoned the hemispheri-cal in favour of the conical stern.

In America, the Baldwin airship has achieved considerable success, and has been adopted by the United States army. It has a pointed stem and stern; a long car attached close to the gas-holder; elevating

THE BALDWIN AIRSHIP.
planes at the fore end, and a vertical rudder at the rear of the car; and a single tractor screw. On its official trials this airship made an independent speed of nearly 20 miles an hour.

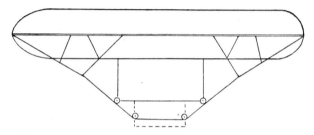

DIAGRAM TO SHOW THE METHOD USED FOR SUSPENDING THE CAR OF "PARSEVAL II".
The cords pass round rollers which allow the car to retain its horizontal position when the balloon tilts.

The list of the world's airships cannot be made complete, as at the time of writing many dirigibles are in course of construction or on trial for all the great Powers. In England a huge rigid airship is being built at Barrow. The Germans have a dozen or more in hand. Russia, Japan, Italy, Belgium, Austria, Spain, and the United States are all busy.

The Continental Tyre Company's fabric is most commonly employed for the gas

MATERIAL USED FOR BALOONS.
chambers of dirigibles. It is built up of four layers. Beginning at the outside, we have - (1) Layer of cotton cloth impregnated with yellow chromate of lead to keep out the actinic (blue to ultra-violet) rays of the sun, which do damage to rubber; (2) layer of vulcanised rubber sheeting to retain the gas; (3) layer of cotton cloth to reinforce that on the outside; (4) thin layer of vulcanised rubber to protect the cotton against the chemical action of the hydrogen gas. In the Gross airships this layer is dispensed with.

The four-layer fabric weighs slightly under ten ounces per square yard. A strip one foot wide will bear a strain up to 950 lbs. before tearing. The two layers of cotton cloth are laid diagonally to one another, so that the warp of one may resist ripping in the weft of the other, and localise injuries to the fabric.

Nulli Secundus II, the very moderately successful British army airship, had a bag built up of many layers of gold-beater's skin, a very tough and impermeable but also very expensive material.

There is no denying the fact that, whereas the development of and interest in the flying machine have been due largely to what one may call the sporting

THE DIRIGIBLE IN WARFARE.
instinct, the dirigible balloon is considered primarily to be an instrument of war. The value of being able to see and give information of what the enemy is doing, without incurring great risks, is of such value to a military commander that in the next great war the dirigible balloon will certainly be very fully tested. In rough weather it will be of no more use than the ordinary spherical balloon, but that fact will not prevent its being kept ready for ascent under favourable conditions. As for the danger from gun fire, this would be minimised by rising to great heights, and one cannot imagine a dirigible being employed that was not capable of ascending 5,000 to 6,000 feet above the earth's surface, if it had to be sent directly over the enemy's position. Even a much less height would allow its passengers to make observations, while keeping out of range. In the grim business of war bold spirits would not be wanting to take heavy risks on the chance of winning through - to play the counterpart of the naval scout. For several years to come, however, the dirigible will be used for observation only, not for dropping explosives or incendiary substances. Possibly a dirigible may have to attack the aircraft of the opposing forces, and to that end might be furnished with small guns, but

it would take no part as combatant in a general engagement. As for aerial invasions - great numbers of men wafted through the air on to the enemy's country - they will not happen for many years to come.

The military value of airships was tested at this year's manoeuvres of the French and German armies, *La République* and *Gross II* being selected for the purpose by the respective Governments. The Gross II got within rifle range, and was ruled out of action, but subsequently was "restored" to her side and did good work. The République managed to get over the "enemy" during a thick mist, and when the latter cleared away, and while the troops below were gaping in astonishment, feeling like partridges under a hawk, those on board took full and accurate notes of the disposition of the attacking forces and sailed away.

ENGINES OF "ZODIAC III".   *(Photo, Topical.)*

The flying machine has also to be taken into consideration. When it is able to rise to heights comparable with those of a balloon, and maintain its elevation for an hour or two at a stretch, it will be practically safe. Its small size and speed will render the chances of its being hit, even by guns that could reach it, quite negligible. We may fitly close this side of the subject with the weighty words of Sir Hiram Maxim: "The value of a successful flying machine, when considered from a purely military standpoint, cannot be over-estimated. The flying machine [we may add the navigable balloon] has come to stay, and whether we like it or not, it is a problem that must be taken into serious consideration. If we are laggards, we shall unquestionably be left behind, with a strong probability that before many years have passed over our heads we shall have to change the colouring of our school maps."

RECORDS OF DIRIGIBLE BALLOONS.

Date.	Name.	Place.	Type.	Duration of Flight.	Distance.	Remarks
1852 Sept. 24.	Giffard's.	Paris.	Non-rigid.	......	......	Velocity, 5 miles per hour. First power - driven dirigible.
1884. Aug. 9.	La France. (Renard & Krebs.)	Meudon, France.	,,	......	......	First practical dirigible to return to starting-point. Velocity, 10 miles per hour.
1885. Sept. 23.	,,	,,	,,	......	......	Velocity, 14 miles per hour.
1898. July 2.	Zeppelin I.	Friedrichshafen, Germany.	Rigid.	1 hr. 20 min.	......	Velocity, 16 miles per hour.
1902. Oct. 19.	Santos Dumont VI.	Paris.	Non-rigid.	30 min. 40 sec.	7 miles.	Circled Eiffel Tower ; won Deutsch Prize.
1903. May 8.	Lebaudy.	Moisson, France.	Semi-rigid.	1 hr. 36 min.	23 miles.	Velocity, about 20 miles per hour.
May 15.	,,	,,	,,	1 hr. 41 min.	38½ miles.	,,
June 24.	,,	,,	,,	2 hr. 46 min.	60 miles.	,,
1905. July 3.	,,	Moisson—Meaux.	,,	2 hr. 37 min.	89 miles.	First stage on journey to eastern frontier.
July 4.	,,	Meaux—Sept Sorts.	,,	47 min.	11 miles.	Second stage on journey to eastern frontier.
July 6.	,,	Sept Sorts—Châlons.	,,	3 hr. 25 min.	61 miles.	Third stage on journey to eastern frontier. Balloon collided with a tree, and was destroyed.
Nov. 10.	,,	Toul, France.	,,	......	......	Reached height of 4,500 ft.
1906. Oct. 10.	Zeppelin III.	Friedrichshafen.	Rigid.	2 hr. 17 min.	69 miles.	
1907. Sept. 30.	,,	,,	,,	8 hr.	211 miles.	Velocity, 35 miles per hour.
Oct. 5.	Nulli Secundus.	Aldershot—London.	Non-rigid.	3 hr. 25 min.	50 miles.	Velocity, 12 miles per hour.
Oct. 28.	Parseval I.	Berlin.	,,	6 hr. 25 min.	......	......
Oct. 28	Gross I.	,,	Semi-rigid.	8 hr. 10 min.	......	......
Nov. 23	La Patrie.	Paris—Verdun.	,,	6 hr. 45 min.	146 miles.	Velocity, 26 miles per hour.
1908. Jan. 15.	Ville de Paris.	,,	Non-rigid.	7 hr. 6 min.	146 miles.	......
July 1.	Zeppelin IV.	Friedrichshafen.	Rigid.	12 hr.	236 miles.	Circular journey over Switzerland.
Aug. 4.	,,	Friedrichshafen—Oppenheim.	,,	11 hr. (first stage only).	258 miles.	Destroyed at Echterdingen on way back to base.
Sept. 11.	Gross II.	Tegel—Magdeburg—Tegel.	Semi-rigid.	13 hr. 15 min.	176 miles.	Reached height of 4,000 ft.
Sept. 15.	Parseval II.	,,	Non-rigid.	11 hr. 32 min.	157 miles.	......
Oct. 6.	Lebaudy.	Moisson.	Semi-rigid	......	......	Reached height of over 5,000 ft.
Oct. 22.	Parseval II.	Tegel.	Non-rigid.	......	......	Maintained height of 5,000 ft. for over an hour.
1909. May 29–31.	Zeppelin II. (New).	Friedrichshafen—Bitterfeld—Göppingen.	Rigid.	37 hr. 40 min.	603 miles.	Record duration and distance. On landing, the dirigible was damaged, but continued its journey to Friedrichshafen.
Aug. 4.	Gross II.	Berlin—Apolda—Berlin.	Semi-rigid.	16 hr.	290 miles.	
Aug. 23.	Clément-Bayard.	Sartrouville, France.	Non-rigid.	......	......	Remained for two hours at height of over 4,000 ft.

[*We have pleasure in acknowledging the help given in the preparation of these articles on aeronautics by the Aeronautical Society of Great Britain ; Mr. T. W. Clarke ; and Mr. H. Ledeboer, Editor of " Aeronautics."*]